30/10/92

DERBYSHIRE IN THE CIVIL WAR

Sir John Gell

The original engraving is held in Derbyshire County Council's Local Studies Library, 22b Irongate, Derby

DERBYSHIRE
in the
CIVIL WAR

BRIAN STONE

SCARTHIN BOOKS
1992

Published by Scarthin Books of Cromford 1992

ISBN 0 907758 58 4

Phototypesetting, printing by
PRINTHAÜS BOOK CO. LTD.
NORTHAMPTON

Contents

Introduction

The story of Derbyshire's involvement in the Civil Wars has not, to date, been published in book form. Of course, various local archaeological and Local History Societies have produced a substantial number of articles and papers, but these have never been collated and logically arranged into a complete narrative. This is surprising; although the County never saw large scale military operations, as, for instance, did Yorkshire, or Nottinghamshire, its strategic importance made it a linchpin of the Parliamentary cause in the Midlands. For the same reason it was a constant target of efforts mounted from the Royalist strongholds of Yorkshire and Northumberland, the Welsh Borders, and the King's capital at Oxford. Possession of Derbyshire, and particularly the important crossings of the River Trent, would effectively have linked these three areas and enabled the Royalists to exert considerable pressure on the Paliamentarian areas of East Anglia and the northern Home Counties. That this was never achieved undoubtedly hastened the demise of the Royalist cause, compelling them to fight on extended lines of communication and making it difficult, if not impossible, to co-ordinate the movements of the various field armies.

Derbyshire was, from the first, a Parliamentary stronghold. In large measure this was due to the efforts of Sir John Gell, the energetic and ruthless governor of Derby during the whole of the First Civil War. Gell's career in itself would fill a book; indeed, a full-length biography is probably overdue. We cannot, in the space of this book, consider it in detail, but his activities bulked so large in the County's affairs that the events of years 1642–1646 were effectively controlled and directed by him. Of necessity, therefore, the history of that period largely parallels Gell's own. After 1646 his involvement ceases, but it is significant that no other single figure appears thereafter to dominate the county scene. Gell stands head and shoulders above the rest as the dynamo of parliamentary activity, and his departure leaves one with a sense almost of anti-climax, so vigorous and pervasive was his presence.

Having thus set the scene and introduced the leading player, one is perhaps entitled to ask the reason for the play. The period of the Civil Wars was undoubtedly one of seminal importance in the history of England. It established, earlier than in any other country in Europe, the process of Parliamentary Government and Limited Monarchy that we now enjoy. Perhaps more importantly, it was our first, and only, social revolution, and entitled to rank with the other two great revolutions of modern times, the French and Russian. As such, it has received a great deal of attention from historians starting with Clarendon's monumental "A History of the Great

Rebellion", through polemics of the Whig Historians to the present more analytical approach of such historians as Christopher Hill and Robert Ashton.

In recent years there has been an increasing tendency to concentrate on local histories. Until the latter end of the nineteenth century, local histories relating exclusively to the Civil War period were few indeed. The last hundred years has seen an ever-increasing number, so that now the majority of counties, and many cities, can lay claim to their own histories of this epoch-making period. Of the counties immediately adjoining Derbyshire, virtually all have at least one history of the Civil Wars. "Staffordshire in the Great Rebellion", "Nottinghamshire in the Civil War", "Lancashire and the Great Civil War", and "The Civil War in Cheshire" cover four of the neighbouring counties. Yorkshire has no general history, but innumerable local ones relating to particular areas of the County. Leicestershire wholly lacks a County history, but even they have one relating to Loughborough. Derbyshire stands alone as entirely lacking a comprehensive book on the period, and it is high time this was remedied.

It is right to say at once that this history does not pretend to be a great work of original research. I have had to be content with a synthesis of previously published material, some of it now scarce and long out of print. No great revelations may therefore be expected, but I hope I have succeeded in combining the various sources into a coherent and readable whole. I have also tried to fit Derbyshire into the overall pattern of events in the country as a whole since incidents in individual counties have little significance unless they are explained in the light of the national events of the time; but in that context they can be extremely important.

My personal justification for writing this book, if one is needed, is quite simple; I find the period absorbing and make no apologies if my enthusiasm occasionally shows through. Seventeenth century man was in many respects a quite different animal from you and me; "he spoke", as one writer put it, "with a deeper voice". But he also shared with us many of the same anxieties, emotions, hesitations and contradictions. Nothing shows this more clearly than the polarisation of civil war; friends and neighbours one day may be killing each other the next. The transformation of their attitudes is what makes the Great Civil War so compelling and instructive.

In short, I hope this book will be enjoyable, to amateur historians and others interested in the history of their County. If the reader finds reading it half as interesting and exciting as I did writing it, I will feel myself amply rewarded.

A word about the title; I was undecided at first whether to call the book "The Civil War in Derbyshire" or "Derbyshire in the Civil War"; it did not take long to choose the latter title since the book is not just about what happened within the confines of the county boundary. The influence of Derbyshire extended into all the surrounding counties, and Derbyshire men fought in many engagements from Edinburgh to Marston Moor, where many were killed. To ignore them and the part they played would be not only churlish, but misleading.

Finally may I express my gratitude to all those who have helped me over the ten years that it has taken to produce this modest work. There are too many to mention all by name but I must acknowledge my wife's unstinting patience during the many hours that I have spent living in the Seventeenth Century! I also owe a great debt to the pioneering work of Dr. Trevor Brighton without whose excellent publications this book would have been impossible, or at least much more difficult, to write. I am uneasily aware that had he been writing this book he would probably have done a much better job. Any errors, of fact or opinion, are, of course, entirely my own.

1 Derbyshire in 1640

They are a bold, daring and even desperate kind of fellows in their search into the Bowels of the Earth .... and therefore they are often entertained by our Engineers in the Wars to carry on the Sap, and other such works, at the Siege of strong fortified places.
Defoe on Derbyshire lead miners.

Derbyshire in the early part of the seventeenth century was in many respects so unlike the county that we know today that some indication of its social, economic and geographical backgound is essential in order to understand the course of the Civil War within and around it; the influence that it exerted in adjoining counties and, indeed, on the course of the war as a whole.

According to Blaeu's Map of 1648, the boundaries of the county were then much as they are now. It was divided into six "hundreds", High Peak, Scarsdale and Wirksworth in the north and east, Appletree, Morleston and Litchurch, and Repton and Gresley in the south and west. Curiously, parts of the hundred of Morleston appear to have lain outside the county boundaries proper, islets of Derbyshire in the midst of adjoining Leicestershire, an anomaly eliminated only in the nineteenth century. Topographically, too, the terrain then was similar; bleak and open moorland in the Peak, fertile and cultivated farmland in the Trent and Derwent Valleys and towards the Nottinghamshire border. In almost every other particular, however, the county of today has only the slightest resemblance to the Derbyshire of 350 years ago.

People give life to landscape, and in the Derbyshire of the 1630s there were vastly fewer of them. It is always a difficult task to assess population growth and distribution at so early a period. The National Census which now provides such material did not come into existence until 1801, so we are dependant upon less accurate data, compiled for quite other reasons, such as the Militia Returns and the Hearth Tax Assessments. These are sufficient, however, to give a reasonable, broad indication of both size and distribution. In the Militia Return for 1631, the number of able-bodied men in the county is given as 15,672. Allowing for women, children and the disabled, it has been estimated that the total population was probably in the region of 45,000. This seems a little on the low side. A Return of Conformists, Nonconformists and Papists in 1676 gives a total for the whole county of 48,657 souls (excluding children under 16). Given the large families usual at that time, and allowing for some loss of life and mobility of population during the Civil War, my own estimate is that the county contained some 60,000 people at the outbreak of hostilities in 1642.[1] It will be readily apparent, therefore, that, by present day standards, the population was extremely sparse, only some 40 persons to the square mile, and, moreover, they were distributed in a pattern almost the reverse of the present day. The area of the High and Low Peak, now relatively thinly inhabited, was then a bustling hive of activity and industry, an activity based almost wholly upon one commodity, lead. There is a vivid description of Wirksworth some sixty years later in Defoe's "A Tour Through the Whole Island of Great Britain".

> "The inhabitants are a rude boorish kind of people, but they are a bold, daring and even desperate kind of fellows in their search into the Bowels of the Earth; for no people in the world outdo them; and therefore they are often entertained by our Engineers in the Wars to carry on the Sap, and other such works, at the Siege of strong fortified places."

The history of lead mining in Derbyshire has a long and honourable pedigree. The Romans first mined lead in the county in the second and third Centuries AD, and Derbyshire lead was in great demand to provide the plumbing for the Romano-British villas, of which there are still remains to be seen in the county. Mining was continued and improved in medieval times, and by the early seventeenth century the Derbyshire lead mines were one of the country's most important mineral producing areas, providing over half of the national tonnage. The only field remotely to rival Derbyshire was that in Somerset, and by 1642 some 20,000 people were directly involved in its production in the Hundreds of High Peak and Wirksworth, perhaps one-third of the entire population of the county.

The effect of lead mining on the social and economic structure of the county is as yet little researched, and imperfectly understood. In a recent thought-provoking article, however, it has been suggested that the widespread exploitation of lead mines and the ownership of the smelting facilities that were a necessary consequence "undermined older power structures and produced increasing conflicts of interest among different segments of Derbyshire Society" contributing to the early breakdown of the county into "two warring factions" at the outbreak of Civil War.[2] Whether this is an accurate reflection or not is a matter for argument, and is not wholly borne out by the political events leading up to the war, or the structures of county society as we understand them. It is undeniable, however, that the exploitation of lead created intense personal, social and political rivalries, particularly in the immediate pre-Civil War period. For one thing, the economic value of the lead fields caused tensions with the Crown. The Hundreds of Wirksworth, High Peak, Repton and Gresley and Appletree, which included the whole of the lead producing area, were all controlled by the Duchy of Lancaster and as such counted as Crown lands. In addition, the Crown also had direct control of no less than 26 Manors within this area. The period of Charles I's personal rule, from 1629 until the Long Parliament of 1641, involved the King in never-ending and only partially successful attempts to raise revenue without Parliamentary authority. One obvious and lucrative source of money was the royalties, known as "fother", on lead produced on Crown lands. In this period the royalty more than doubled from 20 shillings to 48 shillings, until reduced to its original level by the Long Parliament. Leaseholders of mines also paid a rent to the Crown known as "Lot and Cope" but given that the price of lead increased by 50% between 1608 and 1635, this no longer represented an acceptable return. The King therefore granted leases to entrepreneurs to develop mines directly on his behalf, and such men were not always scrupulous about their methods. In 1630, for instance, the King granted Letters Patent to Sir Robert Heath to develop the Dovegang Rake at Middleton, the largest man-made shaft in the county at the time, but then lying idle through flooding. His partner in this enterprise was the famous Dutch engineer, Sir Cornelius Vermuyden, who had incurred the hatred of the Fen-dwellers in his drainage of the marshlands of Lincolnshire and North Nottinghamshire.

The drainage and development of the Dovegang Rake brought these men into conflict with local yeomen and lesser gentry who already owned the rights to adjoining mines. Several of them were forcibly dispossessed, a prime mover in this being one John Molanus, a servant of Vermuyden's of whom we shall hear much more.

By this period, however, the mining interests within the county were sufficiently strong and influential to oppose what they saw as arbitrary or oppressive attempts to change their well-established liberties. The lead miners, in common with other areas of mineral production (e.g. the Stannaries), had gradually accumulated a body of customary law to regulate their relationship with landlords, mine owners and between themselves. They had their own court, the Barmote[3], and a Judge, the Barmaster, who was usually appointed by the Crown. And undoubtedly they needed it; mining appears to have been a source of litigation such as would delight the heart of any lawyer, and the records of the time are full of petitions, actions, complaints and law-suits concerning the right to mine, payment of rent, miners' wages and the like. Many of the Derbyshire gentry had, by this time, become involved in the industry, including many names we shall meet again, both Royalist and Parliamentary. The Gell family of Hopton, for instance, had extensive mining interests in the the Wirksworth area, as did the newly ennobled Cavendish family, the Harpur-Crewes and the Eyres of Hassop. Even as early as the 1590s, about one-third of the "top" 25 families in the county had lead interests of one kind or another, and by the time of the Civil War, perhaps as many as half.

Although the most important commodity, however, lead was not the only one. Small amounts of tin and silver were produced and fairly large amounts of iron-ore, particularly in the eastern part of the county. Coal was also mined, but had not then reached its later importance, most of the national production being concentrated in the coastal mines of Newcastle on Tyne.

The importance of a concentrated and highly developed industry within the county boundaries, however, must not obscure the fact that, like most of early seventeenth century England, Derbyshire was still predominantly agricultural. The poor soils of the North and West Moorlands were given over mainly to the grazing of sheep and to the growing of small amounts of rye, peas and oats, while the fertile flood plains of the Trent and Derwent produced most of the county's cattle, wheat and barley. Indeed, the county was self-sufficient in food and exported a small surplus. In some areas, enclosure was already far advanced. In 1630 the Privy Council ordered returns from all Justices of the Peace concerning the state of enclosure in their Hundreds and the conversion of available land to pasture. In that year the Appletree Justices reported "the great part of this Hundred hath been enclosed long since" and the Wirksworth Justices echoed those comments the following year when they said "most of our Wapentake hath been long since enclosed".[4]

The market for agricultural produce in the south of the county was the county town of Derby, then a thriving community of some 3,000 people. The first known map of the town was published by John Speed in 1610 as an inset to his map of the county and shows a compact little town on the right bank of the Derwent, dominated at its centre by the Church of Allhallows. Its trades were centred on brewing and leathermaking and it had a substantial monthly horse market and a regular cereal and cattle market. Established since Saxon times, when it was called Northworthy, by the early seventeenth century it was very much the commercial and administrative centre of the county; and its situation on the Derwent, then a major transportation route, relieved it of the isolation suffered by so much of the hinterland. In 1637 Charles I granted the town a new charter "for its better government"; the town officials comprised a Mayor, nine Aldermen, fourteen Brethren and fifteen Capital Burgesses, plus a High Steward, Recorder and Town Clerk.[5] This relatively sophisticated system was to provide the basis for the Committees which governed both town and county during the Civil War.

The only other towns of importance in the county were Chesterfield, then as now, the second largest with a population of about 1500, and Bakewell. Buxton had yet to achieve the growth in size and importance that the 18th Century would bring, and its mineral waters were unknown outside the county.

Transport in Derbyshire, as in most of the rest of the country, was a major problem. Roads were few and poor. The main land routes in the county were Roman roads, the most important of which was the Rykneild Way, running north-east into Yorkshire and south-west towards Bath.[6] Other routes were provided by the roads to Nottingham and Lincoln and Burton-on-Trent and Uttoxeter. The remaining roads were either rudimentary or non-existent. In winter even the main roads were frequently made impassable by snow in the High Peak and mud elswhere, and in spring much of the county was subject to severe flooding when the Peak snows melted, pouring into the Dove and the Derwent. The main method of transport was by water along the Trent, where heavy or bulky items could be moved relatively easily. Derbyshire lead was transported by barge along the river and thence to the Humber estuary and the county's main entrepot at Hull. From here the lead was shipped to London and the Continent, the same route being used to export the other main items produced by the county such as unprocessed Derbyshire wool, wheat and ale. Manufactured items that the county could not produce were shipped in along the same route. So important were these routes that they gave rise to considerable friction and jealousy between neighbouring towns. For instance, Nottingham prevented for many years the improvement of navigation along the Derwent so as to maintain its monopoly and consequent toll income from the Derbyshire goods passing through Trent Bridge.

Socially the structure of the county is open to conflicting interpretations, but appears broadly in line with the national average, with some interesting local variations. At the bottom of the pyramid were the landless day labourers, either in agriculture or the lead mines, whose rates of pay were regulated by statute. The wages of an agricultural day labourer in Derbyshire in 1634 were 6d per day.[7] Next above came yeoman farmers and artisans, then merchants and finally the county gentry, great and small, who were the main repository of social, economic and political power. That power derived, in great measure, from the ownership of land, and in that respect Derbyshire was no different from other areas of seventeenth century England. It has been suggested that lead mining in the county meant that the ownership of land (rather than its exploitation under a mining lease) was not essential to wealth and led to a more open society in Derbyshire than elsewhere.[8] This is doubtful. It is certain, however, that virtually all the Derbyshire families who achieved local or national prominence in the first third of the seventeenth century were also possessors of landed estates. By the 1590s the county gentry numbered some 200 families frequently related to each other by blood or marriage in a complex web of relationships. Many of these families had been established in the county for generations, but the early years of the seventeenth century saw a shift in power from the "old" families to new ones. The Talbot family, the Earls of Shrewsbury, whose interests had dominated the county since the early part of the sixteenth century, were waning and the creation of the Earldom of Devonshire in 1618 brought to prominence the Cavendish family, who will play a large part in this story, and continue, to the present day, as one of the largest single landowners in the county. Such changes in structure were not unique to Derbyshire. Recent research has demonstrated that the late Tudor and early Stuart period was one of considerable social and economic mobility. Intermarriage between the gentry of neighbouring counties, the creation of the "new" nobility by James I and the rise of new methods of industrial exploitation all contributed to substantial changes within the gentry classes at large. In Derbyshire this is evidenced by the changing membership of the county government. By 1640, for instance, only Sir John Curzon of Kedleston could claim an ancestor in local office before 1550 and of the Justices of the Peace for the county serving between 1625 and 1640, nearly three-quarters obtained their first appointment to the bench within that period, many owing their increased prominence to the wealth produced by lead mining and smelting interests.[9]

County society, although undergoing a process of change, was still relatively homogeneous in terms of social attitude and religious affiliation. In Derbyshire, however, there was one factor of importance that tended in the other direction, recusancy. In the early years of the seventeenth century, Roman Catholics were still subject to the savageries of the Penal Laws, enacted in the reign of Queen Elizabeth, and in many respects formed their own sub-culture. In certain areas of the country, of which Derbyshire was one, the Catholic community was still of some importance. An agent reporting to Cecil in 1593 described the Peak District as a place "where the papists have their harbours in the stony rocks and are relieved by shepherds so the the county is a sanctuary for all wicked men". The presence of Mary Queen of Scots within and near the county, at Tutbury and in Wingfield Manor, the discovery of the Babington Plot at Dethick and the number of Jesuit priests who found a refuge in the High Peak all led to a considerable persecution of the local Catholic gentry and their tenants. Sir Thomas Fitzherbert, for instance, spent 20 years in gaol for recusancy, and died there, and the three seminary priests, Nicholas Garlick, Robert Ludlam and Richard Simpson, now known as the Padley Martyrs, were hanged, drawn and quartered at Derby in 1588. After Lancashire and the North Riding of Yorkshire, Derbyshire, particularly the Peak District, was probably one of the most Catholic counties in England. By the first quarter of the seventeenth century, the worst of the persecution was over, but harassment continued, albeit exacting less drastic monetary penalties. At the Lent Assizes for the High Peak in 1616, for instance, no less than 210 persons were indicted for recusancy, and 92 convicted and in 1634 the Constable's returns for the High Peak and Scarsdale showed a total of 227 recusants residing there.[10] The area of Hathersage appears to have been almost entirely Catholic, largely due to the influence of the Eyre family. In a recent analysis of the Civil War gentry of Derbyshire, there are no less than 26 Catholics, out of 177 persons identified by name, more than 14% of the total.[11]

By and large a surprising number of Catholic gentry of Derbyshire managed to preserve both their estates and their religion, by a judicious mixture of compromise, influence and deception. Some even managed to achieve considerable standing in the county; Thomas Eyre of Hassop, for instance, was appointed High Sheriff in 1621, raising questions in Parliament and, when indicted at Derby Assizes for recusancy in 1626, he promptly took the Oath of Supremacy and sued his accusers for defamation. This classic example of "Church-Papism" helped to preserve the Eyre estates until well after the Civil War; in 1662 Thomas Eyre's son Rowland, who had fought for the King throughout the Civil War, was said to be worth still some £3,000 per annum, a considerable sum of money in those days.

At the other extreme, evidence of puritanism in Derbyshire is difficult to find. At least one of the county Petitions was couched in puritanical language and some notable members of the county gentry, such as the Curzons and the Gells, were Presbyterian in sympathy, but there appears to be little of the puritan sentiment and iconoclasm that affected London and parts of East Anglia and the Home Counties. Although Derbyshire was in the Diocese of Lichfield, there was no Cathedral within the county then and therefore, perhaps, no focus for discontent with the established church such as existed elsewhere. Furthermore, the holdings of Church land within the county were relatively small. Certainly there were puritan divines such as Emmanuel Bourne of Ashover, but their influence appears to have been relatively slight; much of this would change with the Civil War, but the Derbyshire of 1640 appears to have been averagely Anglican and conformist in its religious adherence.

This, then, was the picture presented by the county in the years immediately preceding the Civil War; largely agricultural, isolated by its poor communications and terrain, relatively poor, with no particular religious extremes, a substantial community of Catholics, a large body of well-established gentry, dependent on landed estates, and one industry of crucial importance, by which the position of the gentry was in large measure supported. All these factors would influence the allegiance of the county in the coming hostilities.

2 The Gathering Storm

No man can show me a source from which these waters of bitterness we now taste have more probably flowed, than from this unseasonable, unskilful and precipitate dissolution of parliaments.
Clarendon on the outbreak of the Civil War.

Charles I ascended the throne of England in 1625, and in 1629 embarked on the 11 year period of what is known as "the personal rule"; it is beyond the scope of this work to discuss the manifold and complex reasons for this fateful decision. Suffice it to say that the parliaments of his first four years were riven by conflicts over a number of fundamental constitutional and

Decimo septimo die Februarij Anno Dom 1640.
County of Derbie

A note of the severall hundreds as they are assessed and have alreadie paid the Shipmoney

	li	s	d
The Hundred of Appletree	617	7	0
The Hundred of Repton and Gresley	442	8	0
The Hundred of Morleston and Litchurch	491	12	0
The Hundred of the Wapentage Wirksworth	357	7	0
The Hundred of Scarsdale	854	18	10
The Hundred of the high Peake	514	8	4
	3278	1	2
The Nobility	120	0	0
The towne of Derbie	175	0	0
The Clergie	108	10	6
	403	10	6
Soma total	3681	11	8

An account of the Ship Money paid by the six Hundreds of Derbyshire and by the nobility, the clergy and Derby itself

Derbyshire Record Office D 258m/31/33g. From the archives of the Chandos-Pole-Gell Family, deposited in Derbyshire Record Office.

religious questions; amongst these was included the levying of unparliamentary revenues, notably Tunnage and Poundage, arbitrary arrest and imprisonment without cause, and the attempts of the King to enforce religious uniformity within the Church of England in the face of an increasingly powerful puritan sentiment. Charles dissolved his fourth parliament on 10th March 1629, and Clarendon noted in retrospect "no man can show me a source from which these waters of bitterness we now taste have more probably flowed, than from this unseasonable, unskilful and precipitate dissolution of parliaments".

Given that revenue was normally raised by Parliamentary grant, Charles's most urgent problem was to find enough money, by extra-parliamentary means, to support his annual expenditure of £600,000 and to finance the national debt, which then stood at £1,000,000.

Even before the dissolution, Charles's attempts to raise revenue outside parliament created friction, and produced only a lukewarm response. In 1626, for instance, he attempted to impose a "benevolence" or free gift on the county, but this met with little success. In Derbyshire the Justices of the Peace, who were responsible for collection, obtained only £20–4–0 from Appletree and Wirksworth, nothing from the other hundreds, and contributed only £91 themselves which, they reported diffidently, was "nothing answerable either to our desires or his Majesty's occasions".[1] Other methods of raising revenue included the sale of baronetcies and other titles, distraint of knighthood (over £40 per annum), the sale of monopolies, customs duties such as Tunnage and Poundage and, of course, the most famous and controversial, the levying of Ship Money.

It had been customary for many years to raise money in coastal counties for the outfitting of royal ships and for protection against piracy. In 1635, however, Charles directed writs for Ship Money to inland counties and when the writs were renewed in the following year it became obvious that the tax was intended to be permanent. The first Ship Money assessment on Derbyshire in 1635 was for £3500, enough to fit out and equip a ship of 350 tons burthen and a crew of 140.[2] The man responsible for its collection was the High Sheriff for that year, John Gell of Hopton (he did not become *Sir* John Gell until 1642) who appears to have collected it with vigour. The impost was levied on the six hundreds of the County, on the Nobility, Clergy and the Corporate Borough of Derby. Derby's assessment stood at £175 and the largest assessment, presumably owing to its lead based wealth, was on the Hundred of Scarsdale (£854–18–10). Initially there was little resistance to the tax and, indeed, the Earl of Newcastle, who had extensive estates in North Derbyshire wrote, with some enthusiasm, "I find myself very ready to pay it and there shall be no failure in the payment". To the Earl, who had spent no less than £15,000 entertaining the King and Queen at Bolsover Castle in 1625, the ship money assessment must have seemed a mere bagatelle. There was, however, one notable defaulter, Sir John Stanhope of Elvaston, who was a justice for the County and related to the Earl of Chesterfield. It appears that Gell had some dislike of Stanhope and he took the opportunity to assess him for what seems to be an excessive sum of £24. Stanhope refused to pay and in what follows we have a foretaste of Gell's attitude to dissent. He distrained upon Stanhope's cattle "starving them in the pound and not suffering anyone to relieve them there".[3] The consequent law suit survived the victim and 18 months later his widow petitioned parliament for redress alleging an over-assessment of her late husband and accusing Gell of peculation. All in all, however, Gell's term as Ship Money collector appears to have been reasonably successful; indeed, he finished with a surplus of funds in hand, reporting to the Ship Money Commissioners, "...there will be some surplussage in my hands which must, according to your Lordships' directions, be distributed back again".[4]

Levies for Ship Money in subsequent years, however, met with an increasingly meagre response. The 1636 assessment was for only £1300, but the then Sheriff John Milward, only managed to collect about half of it. Sir John Harpur of Swarkestone, High Sheriff in 1637, and later a Royalist supporter, did well to collect all save £100 of the 1638 assessment, but the last three years of the Ship Money assessments provoked increasing resistance, particularly from the Borough of Derby, doubtless fortified by its newly acquired Charter, and the last Sheriff, John Agard, met with considerable difficulty in achieving his target.

By 1640 Charles's difficulties were so great that he had no option but to call a Parliament. The catalyst that ended the eleven years of personal rule was renewed war with the Scots, the so-called Second Bishops' War. The spring of 1640 saw feverish activity as the elections for the Short Parliament were arranged. In Derbyshire John Gell took an active part in the preparations on behalf of his step-brother John Curzon who was returned as one of the Members of Parliament for the County, the other being John Manners of Haddon, later 8th Earl of Rutland. In Derby town itself, which also returned two MPs, the Recorder, William Allestree and Alderman Nathanial Hallowes secured election. Allestree was the only one of the four members subsequently to support the Royalist cause, and the election returns in other counties mirrored that of Derbyshire. With such a Parliament the King could expect little satisfaction, and on 5th May the Short Parliament was dissolved.

In the meantime, however, the King had a war to fight and levies were hastily organised up and down the country in order to meet the advancing Scots. In Derbyshire some 400 men were raised to be sent by sea from Grimsby, but the King's rabble of an army were early defeated at the battle of Newburn Ford on 28th August 1640. By the autumn of 1640 the King found it necessary to summon another Parliament (the Long Parliament), which opened on 3rd November 1640. Gell was again active in the elections in which Manvers lost his seat to Sir John Coke the Younger of Melbourne, but Curzon, Hallowes and Allestree were all returned.

The Long Parliament provided that very focus for discontent that Charles had sought so long to avoid, and its proceedings over the next eighteen months are a catalogue of defeats for the King who came under increasing personal and political pressure. The King's closest advisers, Strafford and Laud, were impeached and executed; Ship Money was declared illegal, the Court of High Commission and other arbitrary Crown Courts were abolished, and, most important of all, Parliament passed a Triennial Act and provided that no Parliament should be dissolved without its own consent. Here was proof positive that the personal rule had done nothing to increase the real power of the Monarchy; on the contrary, the simmering resentments of the past eleven years were enhanced and magnified in the heady atmosphere of the House of Commons, dominated as it was by Presbyterian sympathizers, including John Curzon and Nathaniel Hallowes, both of whom were later to sit on the County Committee during the Civil War. Both men signed the Protestation, as did Coke, and the Grand Remonstrance, which rehearsed the grievances of the personal rule. Allestree, significantly, signed neither, and would later join the King's Parliamentary supporters in Oxford at the outbreak of hostilities. By January 1642, it had become obvious to all but the most obtuse that the differences between King and Parliament were irreconcilable and that the parties were on a collision course for war. After his abortive attempt to arrest and impeach five members of the House and faced with the rising hostility of the population of London, Charles left his capital on 10th January and travelled to York. He was never to return, save as a prisoner.

These worrying developments within the Parliament were, throughout late 1641 and 1642, paralleled by equal activity in the provinces as the county gentry sought to exert pressure on Parliament and to sustain the ever-diminishing prospect of a reconciliation with the Crown. It is apparent that, by and large, although many of the Acts passed by their fellows met with the broad approval of the gentry, they were anxious, at the same time, to strike a workable balance between Charles and his Parliament and to avoid the hostilities that appeared increasingly likely, particularly after the King's departure from London. Unlike some more puritan areas, however, Derbyshire was late in formulating its ideas. In neighbouring Nottinghamshire, for instance, petitions to Parliament began as early as the summer of 1641 while Parliament was debating the Root and Branch Bill for the total abolition of episcopacy. In this period Nottinghamshire sent two Petitions to Parliament, one in support and one against, while Kent and other counties did likewise. There is no record, however, that local feeling in Derbyshire produced any petition at that time, and its relative isolation and small parliamentary representation seems to have left it with little influence on events. The departure of the King, however, and the seemingly irreparable breach that it denoted, brought a veritable flood of Petitions from up and down the country.[5]

Derbyshire's first Petition was presented to Parliament on 14th March 1642 by Sir John Curzon on behalf of "divers baronets, knights, esquires, gentlemen, ministers, freeholders and others of the County of Derby" and was signed by over 7000 names.[6] The Petition appears to have been organised by Curzon himself with assistance from his step-brother Gell to whom his friend, the puritan divine Emmanuel Bourne, wrote at the time concerning his "great care and paines besides costs in the last petition". Couched in somewhat puritanical terms, and virulently anti-Catholic, it nevertheless gives an impression of relative moderation; it concluded with what must have been the earnest desire of virtually the whole community of the gentry, that "in the blessed peace of the gospel we may sit every man under his own vine and figtree, and enjoy a happy peace to us and our posterity to the world's end". The content and subscription to county petitions, can however be a misleading index to the strength of support for Parliament. The first Derbyshire Petition was attested by a fairly small proportion of the total population, although many of the gentry signed it. Some of their motives for doing so, however, may be open to question. It would have been difficult, for instance, to refuse to sign a Petition promoted by your landlord or even your father-in law! Furthermore, one suspects that subscribing to the County Petition was rather like voting today; you had to accept the whole package whether you liked all its individual constituents or not. What the Petition does prove, however, is the intense interest and anxiety in the county that was universal elsewhere, whilst any impression of majority support for Parliament can be discounted in the light of later events.

On 19th March the King arrived in York, where he was immediately presented with a Petition from the Nottinghamshire gentry; doubtless prompted by this a letter was written by Sir Francis Rhodes of Barlborough and five other Scarsdale gentlemen to their fellow gentry in the southern hundreds. It read, in part, as follows:

> "This day beinge with some of this side of the countrye, entringe into talke upon report that in some neighbouring counties (as His Majestie hath come along) he hath been humbly sued and petitioned unto, to return back into the south partes and to vouschafe his comfortable present to his Parliament ... we havinge as much reason to take it into consideration as anye other countrey do thinke it not ammisse to moove and desire you the gentry of the other side of this countrey that we may likewise humblye petition his Sacred Majestie for the same favour and happiness (as that would be) if His Majestie would return to his Parliament."[7]

This suggestion met with a ready response from the recipients and a week later the second Derbyshire Petition was drawn up at a meeting at the White Hart Inn in Derby. The original bears 76 signatures, all leading

Front and back views of Sir Francis Rhodes' buff coat. Often worn at this time, the thick leather gave some protection and was lighter than metal armour

From the author's collection

gentry and burgesses, and the signatures included a substantial number of future Royalists as well as the Parliamentary supporters in the County such as Gell, Curzon and the rest. Within the following week copies of the Petition were circulated throughout the county to be signed, and Gell took a leading role in its promotion, writing to the Constable of Mapleton and Thorpe "You are to show this petition to all your nebours and to procure them forthwith to write there names upon this fayre sheet of papp hearwithe sent and to return the same to Sir John Gell before Sundaye nyght next whereof faylle not".[8] The Petition was presented to the King at York on 6th April. A contemporary observer, Joseph Widmerpool of Nottinghamshire, wrote to his brother at the time informing him that it was to be presented by "three hundred at least – the sheriff baronets knights esquires gentlemen and others". Unfortunately, we do not know the King's reaction to it, but we can make an educated guess that it was similar to his response to other County Petitions – to favour it if it supported him and to reject it if it did not. Plainly by now the King had decided, even if the county had not, that the only resolution to his problems would be armed conflict with the Parliament. Indeed, he had already sent Queen Henrietta Maria to France and Holland with the Crown Jewels in order to raise troops, arms and money and his presence at York, where he could rely upon more loyal support than in the capital, was eloquent testimony to his intentions.

The Second Petition was, if anything, even more moderate than the First; it eschewed the outspoken and direct requests of the Nottinghamshire Petition presented some few days before, that the King should listen to his Parliament and dismiss "evil counsellors", and confined itself to a respectful submission that the King should "return and reside neere the Parliament". There is some evidence that Gell disapproved of the moderate tone of the Petition. There is a copy of the Nottinghamshire Petition in his private papers, and his friend Bourne wrote to him after the White Hart meeting "They say you came from Derby before the rest".[9] However that may be, it is clear that even at that late date he and other committed Parliamentarians were still prepared to subscribe to it in the hope that conflict could be avoided. But the time for compromise was past. On 15th February the House of Lords had passed the Militia ordinance, placing the army, such as it was, under the control of Lords Lieutenant appointed by Parliament and on 12th June Charles put into effect his own method of raising troops by appointing "Commissioners of Array" for each county to recruit and train men, provide arms and take over the county magazines. On 15th July the first blood was spilt in an affray over the county magazine at Manchester; in September the King was recruiting men among the Wirksworth lead mines; and by early October, Gell, conveniently absent during the King's stay in the County, was raising a regiment of men in Hull under a Colonel's Commission from the Earl of Essex.

3 Battle is joined

He had not understanding enough to judge the equity of the cause, nor piety, nor holiness; being a foul adulterer all the time he served the parliament, and so unjust, that without any remorse, he suffered his men indifferently to plunder both honest men and cavaliers.
Lucy Hutchinson on Sir John Gell.

Gell plays so crucial a role in the Civil War in Derbyshire that we should, perhaps, pause and consider what manner of man he was. He was born in 1593, the first son of Thomas Gell of Hopton, by his second wife Millicent, daughter of Ralph Sacheverall of Stanton. Within months his father was dead, and his mother had given birth to his brother Thomas. Shortly after, she married John Curzon of Kedleston, where the two Gell boys were brought up, and in 1598 she gave birth to her third son, John Curzon. In

Hopton Hall, the family home of Sir John Gell

Photo: D.J. Mitchell

1610 at the age of 17, Gell went to Oxford, but did not take his degree, returning home to marry his first wife, Elizabeth Willoughby, daughter of Sir Percival Willoughby of Wollaton in Nottinghamshire; by 1620 he was living at Hopton, having inherited his late father's estates, and already had six children, two sons and four daughters. The Gell family had extensive interests in lead mining, and large estates in the Wirksworth area which had been built up piecemeal by successive generations, notably by Gell's father Thomas. By 1624 he had obtained a commission as a Captain of Trained Bands and in 1635 was appointed High Sheriff of the County. Unfortunately no physical description of him appears to have survived, but there are a number of contemporary portraits which depict a man of medium build with a sharp prominent nose, a thin moustache of the accepted early seventeenth century style and a wisp of beard immediately beneath the centre of his lower lip. There is a half portrait of him in armour which oozes vanity from every pore, and although the picture gives no clue as to the height, the set of his shoulders and the arrogant stance, with one arm akimbo, combines to give the impression of a man below average height. This is partially confirmed by the size of his buff coat which survives, and indicates a man perhaps a little over five foot tall. His character accorded closely with his appearance, and it is clear from his actions during the next four years that he was a ruthless and vindictive self-seeker, without scruple in betraying former friends if that would serve his ends; Mrs. Hutchinson describes him thus:

> "He himself, no man knows for what reason, he chose that side (the Parliament); for he had not understanding enough to judge the equity of the cause, nor piety nor holiness; being a foul adulterer all the time he served the parliament, and so unjust, that without any remorse, he suffered his men indifferently to plunder both honest men and cavaliers; so revengeful, that he pursued his malice to Sir John Stanhope ... with such barbarism after his death, that he, pretending to search for arms and plate, came into the church and defaced his monument that cost six hundred pounds ... He dug up a garden of flowers, the only delight of his widow, upon the same pretence; and then wooed that widow ... till, being deluded by his hypocracies, she consented to marry him and found that was the utmost point to which he could carry his revenge, his future carriage making it apparent he sought her for nothing else but to destroy the glory of her husband and his house ... He was a very bad man, to sum up all in that word, yet an instrument of service to the parliament in those parts."[1]

Harsh words indeed, so it should be remembered that the writer had a personal axe to grind: her husband's first wife was Sir John Stanhope's daughter, a classic instance of the close connections between the local county gentry. Actions speak louder than words, and the reader may draw his or her own conclusions as to Gell's character from his conduct as

Governor of Derby and later. It is plain, however, that whatever his vices he was a man of considerable efficiency, vigour and force of character, as his actions as High Sheriff and in the promotion of the Derbyshire Petitions had already shown, and Parliament was in dire need of such men at that time, for Derbyshire was an area of considerable strategic importance. As for his alleged womanising, he is reputed to have said "I never meddle with women, unless they be handsome!" Make of that what you will!

At a time when roads were at best rudimentary, the most important means of inland transport was by river, and far and away the most important navigable waterway in eastern England was the Trent. A glance at the map will show that it virtually bisects the eastern half of the country from Burton to its estuary at Hull and Hull was then one of the main ports of the entire country, drawing the produce of the inland counties to itself along the river and exporting them to London and the Continent. The control of river lines, than as now, was a matter of prime military importance, particularly as the Trent formed not only a means of communication but a barrier to military operations, and Derbyshire controlled the two most important crossing points on the whole of the upper reaches of the river, by ferry at Wilne (what is now Shardlow), and by bridge at Swarkestone. By October 1642, the King would have occupied Oxford, his capital for the next four years. From here he would be able to draw recruits from the Royalist areas of Wales, and the Welsh marches. His other main area of support, however, was in Yorkshire and the two northern-most counties of Northumberland and Durham; if the King could unite his two field armies, his own at Oxford and the Earl of Newcastle's in Yorkshire, he could effectively outnumber the Parliament's armies at every turn, and defeat them in detail. Prior to this, however, he had first to secure his communications between the two, separated as they were by Derbyshire and Nottinghamshire; whichever side first secured those two vital counties, therefore, would be half-way to winning the war. In Derbyshire's case there were also two further factors of importance; one was the presence of the lead mining industry within her borders, already highly developed and profitable. Not only was this a valuable source of revenue to the protagonists, but it was a commodity which was absolutely indispensable in war – both for the manufacture of musket bullets and for use in gun-founding as an ingredient of gun-metal. Secondly the area of the High Peak and northern hundreds of the county formed a second barrier to communication between the north-east and the south-west Midlands, as the Earl of Newcastle would in time discover.

By mid-June therefore the King had taken steps to recruit and consolidate his position. He sent Henry Hastings to Leicestershire to enforce the Commission of Array, which he proceeded to do, assisted by one hundred coal miners from his father's mines in Derbyshire. The Earl of Rutland countered by convening a meeting of the Justices at the White

Hart Inn at Derby on 29th June. Gell, Curzon and some eight others attended and Parliament was petitioned for permission to array the militia. Within ten days Parliament had authorised the appointment of Militia Commissioners, the first being Sir John Gell and the Earl of Rutland. At about the same time, William Cavendish, Earl of Devonshire, entered Derbyshire from York in order to execute the Commission of Array. On 19th August the King decided to march south, gathering adherents on his journey, and on 22nd August he raised his standard at Nottingham, and war had become inevitable.

The attitude of the county gentry at this time is confusing to say the least, but doubtless the situation seemed equally confusing to them.[2] The first eight months of 1642 had clearly been a period of accelerating movement to war, and one would have expected some polarization of opinion. There had indeed been some tentative taking of sides, but not as much as one might have expected. Even as late as Rutland's Meeting at the White Hart Inn in June, at least half of the signatories of the letter to Parliament were gentry who would later support the King; the recusant baronets John and William Fitzherbert were present, both subsequently Royalist officers of some distinction, as was John Agard of Foston, a lukewarm Royalist who attempted to fortify his house for the King. Curzon and Gell, of course, were present, as was Samuel Sleigh of Ashe, another Presbyterian and later a member of the Parliamentary Committee for the County. The collective action of such disparate personalities suggests that there was still a strong feeling towards neutralism in the county, as the gentry desperately sought to avoid seizing the nettle of decision. So intense was the conflict of motives at this time that it is almost tangible, but by December of 1642, while the King's army recuperated in winter quarters at Oxford, those peaceful aspirations had vanished, and Derbyshire was irretrievably split between King and Parliament. By mid-October, the same Sir John Fitzherbert who had attended the White Hart Inn meeting was signatory to a threatening letter sent to Gell by some of the county gentry from Tutbury admonishing him for appearing in the county with a regiment of foot. The narrative and mechanics of this division into two camps is clear, the motives and psychology less so.

It is a feature of the post-war historiography of seventeenth century England that the gentry had social or economic reasons for choosing one side or the other in the Civil War, and some eminent historians, Trevor-Roper and Christopher Hill, for instance, have sought to demonstrate that the decision rested upon the rise or decline in the material fortunes of the parties. At a local level, Alan Everitt in his closely researched and well presented "The Community of Kent and the Great Rebellion" has analyzed the motives of Royalists, Parliamentarians and Neutrals in one county, and reaches some interesting conclusions.[3] Unfortunately, no such detailed research has been carried out in Derbyshire, and the little that has seems to produce conflicting views. On the basis of present information, however, we may draw some tentative conclusions: firstly, the north and west of the county tended to be more Royalist, whilst the south and east inclined towards Parliament. There are several reasons for this; the northern hundreds contained far and away the largest number of Catholics; if there is one fact that is clear it is that Catholics in the Civil War chose either an uneasy neutrality or sided with the King. In view of the virulently anti-Catholic pronouncements of the Long Parliament, this is perhaps not surprising. In addition, the influence of the Cavendish family in the Pennine area was considerable, and they were all Royalists. It is perhaps to be expected, therefore, that their immediate neighbours among the gentry, who may also have been their tenants, chose the same side. Secondly, the nobility of Derbyshire were Royalist almost to a man, the only exception being the Earl of Rutland, who, in any event, was absent from the county for most of the war. The Cavendish family, William Earl of Devonshire and his cousin William Earl of Newcastle, the eccentric Francis Leake Lord Deincourt and Philip Stanhope 1st Earl of Chesterfield all supported the King. Whilst that is an obvious fact in Derbyshire, however, it has little significance for the country as a whole, where a considerable number of the nobility supported Parliament – the Earl of Essex, the Earl of Warwick, Lord Grey of Grobey and Lord Brooke all held prominent positions in the Parliamentary army and doubtless brought in their tenantry and employees on the same side. Finally, in Derbyshire, as elsewhere, the towns tended to support Parliament and the countryside the King – both Derby itself and Chesterfield were solidly for Parliament and remained so throughout the war, notwithstanding, in the case of Chesterfield, a considerable period of occupation by Royalist forces.[4]

For the rest, there is as yet insufficient evidence to show any connection between the side chosen and the person's material position; gentry with lead mining interests, for instance, chose King or Parliament with equal facility; nor is there substantial reason to believe that an increase or decrease in their prosperity was a central motivating force.

In the last analysis, personal and religious factors were probably crucial to most members of the gentry. Presbyterians would naturally tend to Parliament, Anglicans to the King. In the case of Sir John Gell, it has been suggested that he chose Parliament because his enemies, the Stanhopes, were Royalist; that may well be true, and there is certainly more than a grain of truth in Mrs Hutchinson's assertion that he "so highly misdemeaned himself (over Ship Money collection) that he looked for punishment from the Parliament; to prevent it, he very early put himself into their service". The protection of their personal position was no doubt a compelling motive in the case of at least some of the county community.

Whatever the difficulties of their individual decisions, however, by the end of 1642 most members of the gentry had, more or less reluctantly, chosen sides, as the pressure of events mounted. Some of them did so, however, with a marked lack of enthusiasm. The Earl of Kingston, approached by the King's messengers requesting a loan of "ten or five thousand pounds" replied:

> "that all men knew that he neither had nor could have money, because he had every year...purchased a thousand pounds land a year... But, he said, he had a neighbour who lived within a few miles of him, the Lord Deincourt, who was good for nothing, lived like a hog...and who could not have so little as £20,000 in the scurvy house in which he lived."

The King's men went on to Sutton near Chesterfield, the home of Francis Leake Lord Deincourt and put the same request to him.

> "The lord, with as cheerful a countenance as his could be, for he had a very unusual and unpleasant face, told him; that though he had no money himself but was in extreme want of it...that he had a neighbour the Earl of Kingston, that never did good to anybody, and loved nobody but himself...and could furnish the King with as much as he had need of; and if he should deny that he had money...he knew where he had one trunk full and would discover it."[5]

It is said that the story was related at court with great amusement!

During his two week stay at Nottingham, the King applied himself to recruitment in that county and Derbyshire. His military position at the time was extremely weak. Clarendon describes the reaction of Sir Jacob Astley who informed the King "that he could not give any assurance against his Majesty being taken out of his bed, if the rebels should make a brisk attempt to that purpose".[6] The King had only some 800 horse, most armed only with swords, and his recruiting in Nottingham raised a paltry 300 men, many poorly armed and even worse trained. The Derbyshire lead miners seemed an obvious choice. Many of them worked the lead mines in the King's Field and were, in effect, royal employees. The Master of the King's Mines, Sir Thomas Bushell, was despatched to the Peak to raise recruits and managed to enlist some four thousand, of whom one thousand marched with the King to Shrewsbury and formed the nucleus of his Life-Guard of Foot – this service was later acknowledged by the King in a letter to Bushell. His part in this very considerable service, however, is open to some doubt. At the time of the Restoration, one Thomas Violett petitioned the Crown and alleged that he was the real recruiter.

> "Mr Thomas Bushell can certifie His Majestie, that though he had the name of raising the Derbishire miners, I engaged Mr Fulwood of the Peak, at my request and charge to be chiefly instrumental to get the miners to meet His Majestie at Derby, and was acting with Mr Bushel of Tisdelmore (Tideswell

List of "trayned men; Hundred of Morleiston and Litchurche 1639". Some are armed with a musket, others with bow and pike, though in practice the bow was now obsolete

Derbyshire Record Office D 156m/162. From the Burdett of Foremark Collection, reproduced by permission of Derbyshire Record Office

> Moor) in Derbishire, for the getting of miners together, and there was at one time 1100 souldiers listed at Derby, for which service I received His Majestie's commands, both at York, Nottingham and Derby, about the same time his Majestie set up his standard."[7]

By 13th September the King had recruited his forces sufficiently to move westwards to Shrewsbury away from the growing strength of Parliament in the East Midlands – towards what he hoped would be more fertile ground in the Welsh Marches. On the following day he carried out a review of his forces in Derbyshire, recruited 500 of the County Trained Bands, and dismissed the remainder. On the 15th September he entered Derby with his forces, raised a forced loan of £300 from the Corporation, seized all available small arms and on the following day marched on for Uttoxeter. Gell, in the meantime, had not been inactive. Thinking it prudent to absent himself during the King's stay in Nottingham, and subsequent progress through the county, Gell was with his brother Thomas at Warwick and at Northampton where he procured a Colonel's Commission from the Earl of Essex to raise a foot regiment of 1200 men. The question was where to find them.

The garrison of Hull, with which Derbyshire had had a long-standing relationship as its chief entrepot, had recently been reinforced, and Gell, who went there with his brother in early October, prevailed on the Governor, Sir John Hotham, to provide him with a company of 120 Greycoats from Cawood Castle to act as the nucleus of his regiment. Returning via Sheffield, which they reached on 16th October, they had their first taste of action.

> "And in our way we were importuned to helpe there at Sheffield to suppress a muteny there, which we did, and they lent us ould calivers[8] wyth rotten stocks and rusty barrells, useless to them and of little service to us, for which they seized and took afterwards sixty good muskets[9] of ours, as they came from Hull."

Notwithstanding this unfortunate depletion in his slender armament, Gell's action undoubtedly benefitted the Parliamentary cause in South Yorkshire and he left Sheffield on the following day in a useful posture of defence and in the capable hands of the local commander, Captain Bright. On the same day he reached Chesterfield, where he paused to recruit his strength and review the position.

When the King had departed some four weeks earlier, there was hardly a force in being capable of seizing the county for the Parliament. Indeed, the absence of Gell's invigorating presence and the helplessness of the Parliamentary supporters in the county, devoid as they were of arms, men or leadership, left a void that could easily have been filled by the Royalists, which would have changed the course of the war in the East Midlands and turned it greatly to the King's advantage. Surprisingly, however, little seems to have been done. By the time Gell arrived at Chesterfield, the only Royalist activity of moment was the presence of Sir Francis Wortley at Wirksworth where, assisted by two Royalist officers, Dennis and Ballard, he had recruited a company or so of men and gone into winter quarters. Astonishingly, no attempt was even made to garrison suitable houses or to seize the county magazine at Derby. Such supine indifference would, as always, reap its own reward; viewing the position a month or so later, Clarendon would comment that Derbyshire had left in it "no visible party for the King". And yet things could have been so different; the area was devoid of Parliamentary forces, more than half the county gentry were in varying degrees sympathetic to the King, they had adequate resources of plate and ready money, and a virtual monopoly of the county government. As it was, the first action in the county was a distinct anti-climax. Having raised a further 200 men in Chesterfield, Gell marched to Wirksworth on 26th October and Wortley and his men fled without a fight, leaving Gell to survey his plundered estates in the area, on which he bitterly commented:

> "Major Gilbert Kniveton for a private grudge procured some of his late Majestie's forces to go to my house and plundered it to a third, myself then being out of the county: whither word was sent to me in case I did not come there my skin should be pegged full of bullets."

On 31st October, having raised another 200 miners on his own estates, he marched into Derby and occupied it for the Parliament.

The entry of Gell into Derbyshire roused the Royalist gentry to some action at last. After a meeting at Tutbury, attended by, among others, the Earls of Devonshire and Chesterfield, Sir John Harpur of Calke and Sir John Fitzherbert of Norbury, a letter was sent to Gell at Chesterfield deploring his presence in the County with Parliamentarian troops. Gell returned his usual forthright answer:

> "that it seemed strange that they should grow so quickly jealous of hym, theyre owne countrieman, well known to them, and that had no other end, than the clearing of his county from theeves and robbers, to mayntaine the laws of the land and liberties of the subject, according to the ordynance of parliament, and yet for a long tyme they could suffer Sir Francis Wortley and others to robb and spoyle without interruption."

Immediately upon his entry into Derby, Gell set about securing it and the surrounding countryside. His forces, then standing at some 500, were shortly strengthened by the arrival of Sir George Gresley with a troop of horse, and of Charles White from Nottingham with a small force of 27 dragoons which was soon raised to 140. A committee was formed, and letters was sent requesting contributions to be forwarded to its treasurer,

Nathaniel Hallowes, the only remaining MP for the Borough. Johannes Molanus, commissioned a few days previously by Gell as his Major of Foot, was despatched to Coventry to pick up two sakers[10] and ammunition. Sir John Curzon returned from London to help in the organisation and muskets were sent from London and Hull to arm Gell's Regiment, now almost at full strength. Meanwhile, the elusive Wortley had returned again to Dale, near Wirksworth, to beat-up recruits for the King. Gell sent mounted musketeers and drove him out. But greater threats were in preparation. Philip Earl of Chesterfield met his son Ferdinando with a troop of horse at Burton, and garrisoned his house at Bretby for the King. At the beginning of December Gell sent 400 men under Molanus to besiege it, accompanied by the two sakers recently acquired from Coventry. Although not built for such purposes, the Earl had apparently put it into a reasonable state of defence with earthworks, and his garrison of 40 musketeers and 80 horse[11] were well equipped with ordnance. Initially the Parliamentarians tried the cautious approach, battering the walls with the sakers, but, making no impression, Molanus ordered his men to assault the garrison. The fury of their attack soon overcame resistance and the Earl and his surviving garrison fled towards Lichfield. There are no details of casualties for this action, but it appears to have taken less than a day and they cannot have been very great on either side. Having captured the house, Gell's men immediately set-to to justify Mrs. Hutchinson's description of them as "the most exquisite plunderers", and Gell himself, who was not present in person, was to find himself engaged in yet another personal feud, which would have repercussions later at the Siege of Lichfield Close. His *True Relation* gives a vivid account of what followed.

> "Wee, forsably entring the house, found his Countess, her gentlewoman and two or three servants therein, seized presently uppon the armes, and found seven drakes, thirty steele pikes, twenty or thirty musquetts, five double barrells of powder and good store of match and bulletts. Major Mollanus, Captayne White, Captayne Saunders and divers other officers entreated the Countess that she would give every souldyer halfe a crowne, for to have her saved from plundering, because it was a free boottey. Shee answered, it was too much, and that she had not so much monyes: they asked her again if shee would give amongst them forty marks; shee made the same answer, that shee had not monyes. Then they offered to deposite the money for her, if shee would promise to repay it them: shee still refractoroly and willfully said, that she would not give them one penny; and then indeed the souldyers plundered the house. But the said officers saved her owne chamber, with all the goods therein."

By Christmas of 1642 Gell had disposed of the Royalist forces within the county, for the time being at least, and could turn his attention to the assistance of the Parliamentarian forces in the neighbouring counties of Leicester, Nottingham and Stafford.

4 The Siege of Lichfield and the Battle of Hopton Heath

He speedely gott them into order and gave the enemie such a vollie of shott upon theyre chardge, that they first wheeled, and much discouraged by the death of the Earle of Northampton and captaine Middleton, with dyvers others gentlemen and officers, they all presently Fledd.

Sir George Gresley on Sir John Gell at Hopton Heath.

Gell's defeat of the Earl of Chesterfield at Bretby provided only temporary relief to his as yet untried forces. Henry Hastings, second son of the 5th Earl of Huntingdon, had, in late November, garrisoned Tutbury Castle in response to a request from Sir John Harpur, and some ten days later sent forces to garrison his father's castle as Ashby. Both places presented a constant threat to the south and west of the county throughout the war, and were a substantial help to the King in containing any descent on Oxford and his rear from the North Midlands. Hastings was aged 33 at this time, and was the only Royalist in the area who could match Gell in vigour and enterprise. He had been High Sheriff of Leicestershire in 1642 and was at the Battle of Edgehill on 23rd October as Commander of the 3rd Regiment of the King's Marching Army. The result was indecisive for the King and in early December, after the abortive attempt on London and the storming of Brentford, his army retired into winter quarters; not so Hastings. As soon as he had returned to his native county he threw a regiment into Sir John Harpur's house covering the approaches to the vital Swarkestone Bridge over the Trent. This move caught Gell off-balance. After the skirmish at Bretby he had sent first Captain White and his dragoons to Nottingham, where they had seized all the arms, and then supported him with Major Molanus and three hundred foot, who assisted in the raising of a Regiment for Colonel Pierrepoint and endeavoured to put the town into a defensible state. When Gell heard that Hastings had returned to Ashby with some seven hundred men, he quickly recalled Molanus and his men, and marched in person with his entire regiment to assault the bridge, accompanied by the two sakers which had proved so ineffective at Bretby. On 5th January 1643 an attack was speedily launched against the enemy's works and they were driven off and Harpur's home captured. In their retreat they demolished part of the Swarkestone Bridge, but Gell had good cause to be satisfied with his little victory. At a cost of only one man wounded, he had killed "seven or eight (of them) and wounded many ... soe that the enemy never had a mind to fortifie the same againe". He had also secured the vital Trent crossing and the demolition of part of the bridge, whilst impeding his own movements into Leicestershire and Staffordshire, would likewise hinder the Royalists' approach to Derby.

It is apparent from his own *Relation* that Gell's services were much in demand at this time from the Parliamentary supporters in adjoining counties, and clearly his forces had been more quickly raised and were quicker into action than those in Staffordshire and Nottinghamshire. No sooner had Gell returned from his attack on Swarkestone, than he received a plea for assistance from the Staffordshire Moorlanders who viewed with dismay the increasing Royalist presence in their county. Indeed, the Royalists, under the energetic Hastings, had just occupied Stafford. The redoubtable Major Molanus was immediately sent the eighteen miles to Uttoxeter with 200 musketeers and one of the sakers to succour the Parliamentarians, but waiting there for some days without any support he was forced to retreat back to Derby. Officers were, however, sent to Leek to train the Moorlanders. Hastings, meanwhile (this "thorne in our sydes" as Gell calls him) was busily engaged in strengthening the fortifications of Ashby, and Gell was ordered to join forces with Lord Grey of Grobey and Sir William Brereton for a joint assault on the town. On 15th December 1642, Derbyshire had been joined together with Leicestershire, Nottinghamshire, Northampton, Buckingham, Bedford, Rutland and Huntingdon in the Midland Association under Grey's nominal control. The attack began on 17th January 1643 and the Royalists were quickly beaten from the town itself and retreated into the Church and Castle, Gell's regiment losing four or five killed and one lieutenant wounded. The Parliamentarians trained their guns on the Castle and were about to commence a bombardment when Grey received a letter from the Committee of Northampton warning him that Prince Rupert was on his way to Banbury to relieve the town, "which", says Gell bitterly, "he too easily believed, and called us off and so saved Hastings and the house which otherwise had been yielded to us".

His retreat to Derby afforded Gell little respite from the demands of the desperately undermanned and ill-trained Parliamentarians in the North Midlands. In early February he had to detach Captain Munday's company to assist in the fortification of Sheffield Castle, a garrison had to be provided for Burton on Trent, and Captain Stafford was sent with a company to Whaleybridge to guard the passes from Lancashire, and, no doubt, to co-operate as necessary with Brereton whose forces at the time were concentrated in that area. It was unfortunate, therefore, that the Earl of Essex chose that moment to seek Gell's help on yet another enterprise, the first attack on the Royalist Fortress of Newark. Ever since December of 1642, the Royalists had been busy in fortifying and garrisoning this strategically important town, which controlled the lowest bridge across the Trent and was to pose a constant threat to the Parliamentarian forces in the area.

The garrison was commanded by the veteran Scot, Sir John Henderson, who carried on the works vigorously, and until late February the local Parliamentarians had been too weak and disorganised to do anything to stop him. On 24th February Essex ordered Gell and the local Parliamentarian commanders in Lincolnshire, Nottinghamshire and Yorkshire to send whatever men could be spared for a joint assault on Newark, to be led by Major General Ballard. Doubtless with some irritation, Gell complied, sending the by now much travelled Major Molanus and 500 foot, bringing Ballard's forces up to 6000 men with 10 guns. On 28th February, having advanced his forces towards the town, they beat the enemy from their trenches, losing 4 or 5 men, and entrenched themselves. Gell's troops appear to have been on the western side of Newark with Hutchinson's Nottingham men, while the Lincolnshire forces under Ballard himself were entrenched on the east. For some reason best known to himself, but most probably a lukewarm attachment to the Parliamentarian cause, Ballard ordered part of the Lincolnshire forces under Captain King to retreat, leaving the Derby and Nottingham men unsupported at the mercy of the garrison; Mrs Hutchinson describes what happened:

> "...the whole force of Newark fell upon the forces of Nottingham and Derby, in their trenches, where they fought very resolutely, till a Lincolnshire trooper came and bade them fly for their lives, or else they were lost men. At this, two hundred Lincolnshire men, whom Ballard with much entreaty had sent to relieve them, first ran away, and then Sir John Gell's grey-coats made their retreat after them."[1]

Reporting later to Gell, Molanus told him that "had not Nottingham men and his stood against the said Ballard's will, closely one to another, they had lost all their ordnance, which they fetched off, whether he would or not". As it was, Molanus's men had had to abandon one of their precious drakes[2] to the enemy and lost a number of killed and wounded. How many is unknown, but the Royalists claimed that the total losses to the attackers were 200 killed and many wounded; a reasonable guess for the Derby contingent would be perhaps 50 casualties, and they were men that Gell could ill-spare; by the time Molanus returned with his troops, Gell was already engaged on the far side of the county in the Siege of Lichfield Close.

Chesterfield, having been driven from Bretby, recruited his forces in Lichfield and fortified and garrisoned the Cathedral and Close. The Commander of the associated counties of Warwickshire and Staffordshire,

Robert, Lord Brooke, the Parliamentarian commander killed at the siege of Lichfield

From the author's collection

Robert, Lord Brooke, was ordered from London with a detachment of Essex's army, and on 1st March, assisted by reinforcements from Birmingham, Coventry and Warwick, he began his siege. Within hours of his arrival he was dead, shot in the head by a sniper while surveying the progress of the siege from his lodgings. The disorganised and leaderless Parliamentarians held a Council of War and Captain Fox was sent to Derby to request the indefatigable Gell to take command. He responded promptly, leaving Derby garrisoned only by Captain Mellors and, accompanied by Gresley's troop of horse, he arrived the same day to take over the command. No doubt this additional burden was lightened by the knowledge that his late adversary Chesterfield was in command of the Royalists; showing his usual spirited penchant for a personal feud, Gell immediately offered a reward for the Earl of £100 dead or alive, and Royalist accounts say that he also took as hostage friends and relatives of the garrison and placed them in front of his own assault parties. The real key to the situation, however, was artillery, and Gell sent immediately to Coventry for a mortar. When this arrived on 4th March, it was trained on the Close and lobbed three shells among the garrison, who then called for a parley and surrendered. As Gell entered the Close with his men,

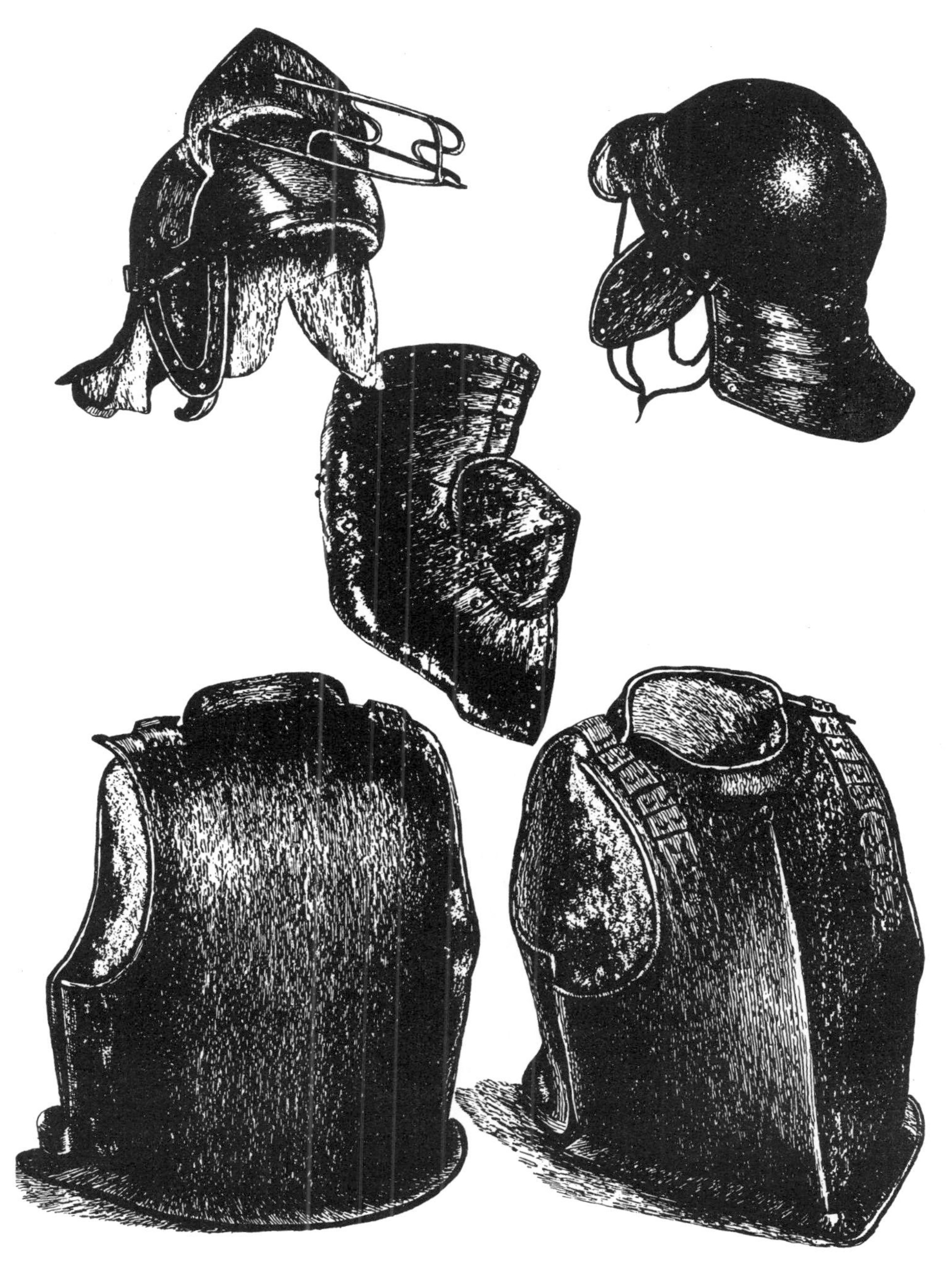

Lord Brooke's armour, showing breastplate and backplate, helmet and elbow-piece for the sword-arm which was particularly vulnerable

From the author's collection

Chesterfield is said to have shouted to some of the women in the garrison "You whores, go down on your knees and give the noble Colonel Sir John Gell thanks for sparing us all". Gell's own account is strangely silent on this, but, if it happened, it doubtless gave him cause for vindictive amusement. The Earl was sent to Wingfield Manor where he remained a prisoner for some months before being sent to London. He eventually compounded for his estates and took no further part in the war.

While garrisoning the Close with some of his own forces, Gell received a letter from Sir William Brereton, then lying at Nantwich, suggesting a joint assault on Stafford. Having failed once before in this, Gell accepted readily and a rendezvous was arranged at Hopton Heath some three miles from the town. The Royalists at Stafford hastened to inform the King at Oxford, who sent Spencer Compton, Earl of Northampton, to their assistance with a detachment of horse and dragoons some 1100 strong and a small body of foot from his garrison at Banbury Castle. Arriving at Stafford on 17th March, the Earl acted with dispatch, attacking some of the Parliamentary horse in their quarters around Lichfield and killing and taking prisoner over a hundred. Gell meanwhile was marching his forces steadily towards Hopton Heath where he arrived on the morning of Sunday 19th March 1643. At that time the Heath, which lay half-way between the villages of Salt and Hopton on the south side of the Trent, was an area of rough open ground enclosed on the west by a large walled hay-field and on the east by the Ingestre Deer Park. Adjoining the Deer Park on its western side was a middling-sized country estate called "The Heathyards" enclosed by a wall which formed a salient into the Heath. Between the Deer Park and the Heathyards ran the road from Stafford, whence Northampton would march, and Weston, through which Gell's troops had come that morning. The Heath itself was uncultivated and was dominated at its narrowest point by a low ridge running east-west, with a rabbit warren in front of the eastern side and a low hill on the west. As Gell moved his troops on to the Heath at about 9.30am, he obviously appreciated the tactical significance of the ground, for he deployed his forces along the ridge to await the arrival of Brereton, in a position which dominated both Brereton's route from Newcastle-under-Lyne and the road from Stafford, while at the same time covering his lines of communication to Weston and Uttoxeter. By now his total strength was about 1500 men comprising perhaps 400 horse of Lord Brooke's Reformado[3] Regiment, his own Dragoons of Gresley's Troop, 500 musketeers, mostly Derby Greycoats returned from the abortive attack on Newark, and perhaps 500 ill-armed Staffordshire Moorlanders, who seemed to have benefitted little from their training by Gell's officers at Leek. He also had a sizeable train of artillery including the mortar used at Lichfield, a culverin, a demi-culverin, 4 sakers and 8 drakes. The mortar would be of little use in the coming battle, but the lighter field pieces would be useful in making up his deficiency in

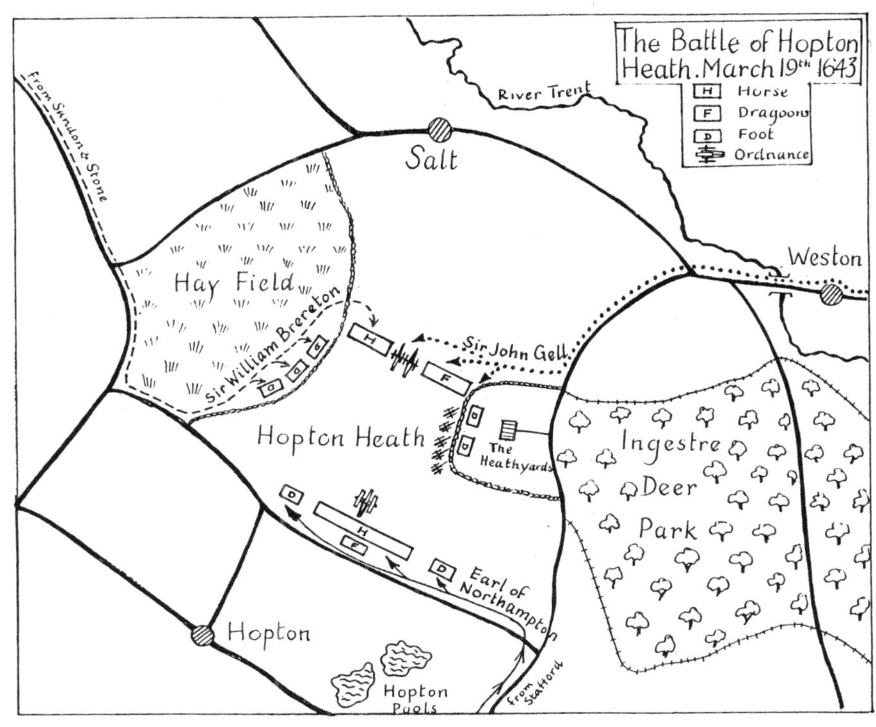

Map of the Battle of Hopton Heath

REPRODUCED BY KIND PERMISSION OF DR TREVOR BRIGHTON

cavalry, and in supporting his dragoons.

Given his lack of formal military training, Gell's deployment of his troops was impressive. He threw some of his dragoons forward behind the walls of the Heathyards, supported by four of his drakes and a "commanded body" of musketeers. His foot was placed on the left wing, protected in front by the rabbit warren, which was unsuitable ground for a cavalry charge. In the centre he positioned his heavier artillery and on the right covering the ground between the hill and the wall of the hayfield he deployed his small body of cavalry. The Moorlanders were positioned at the rear, out of harm's way. The next few hours must have been an anxious time for Gell as he awaited the arrival of Brereton and his forces, and he must frequently have wondered whether Northampton would reach him first and overwhelm his little army. We do not know, of course, how he spent his time, but we do know that he possessed a contemporary drill book *The Pathwaie to Martiall Discipline*; perhaps he read it nervously, checking his dispositions and worrying about the ability of his troops to meet the hardened Royalist cavalry, for Northampton's forces included the Prince of Wales' Regiment, led by Sir Thomas Byron, one of the most dashing (and rash) of the Royalist commanders.

Northampton had been warned of Gell's arrival on the Heath at about 11am whilst he was attending Divine Service at St Mary's, Stafford. Fortunately for Gell, his troops were scattered through the surrounding villages and it was 3pm before they could be deployed to face him south of the ridge in front of the village of Hopton and the Hopton Pools. Brereton had arrived to reinforce Gell about one hour earlier, but in his haste he had had to divest himself of his foot who were still trudging some miles in his rear. He had, however, brought a valuable addition of two troops of horse and three of dragoons, perhaps some 500 men to bring Gell's forces up to about 2000. Brereton quickly lined the flanking walls of the Hayfield with his dragoons and deployed his horse on the Parliamentary right wing in support of Gresley's troopers and the Reformados. Gell took command of the foot, Brereton the horse.

Below, and about 1500 yards away, Northampton faced the Parliamentarians with his force of about 1200 men, only 100 of them foot, and a few guns, including "Roaring Meg", a 29lb demi-cannon. With this he opened the battle with a brisk cannonade, which seems to have done some execution among the Parliamentarians for the first shot "killed six of their men and hurt four, and the next made such a lane through them that they had little mind to close again". The Royalists followed up by clearing their flanks from the cross fire of Gell and Brereton's dragoons ensconced behind the walls and hedges of the Hayfield and the Heathyards, who were driven off with some casualties. On the left wing, Gell's dragoons lost their field pieces. The way was now open for a full-scale attack, and Northampton in person led his cavalry in a vigorous charge on the Parliamentarians' right wing where he routed Brereton's newly arrived horse and took eight of Gell's field pieces. Swiftly reforming his men, he then charged the remaining horse and scattered them after a brisk encounter. Although Gell's foot had not yet been involved, the sight of their horse fleeing before the Royalist onslaught had plainly unsettled them and they were showing signs of panic. Gresley's account tells us what happened next.

> "Our Collonel (Gell) quitt his horse, and went to the foote, being then in great feare and disorder, many of them readie to rune, and standing with theyre pykes advanced; the Colonnel, with his owne hands, put down theyre pykes, encouraged both them and the musquetyers, who were all disorderly crowded together; he speedely gott them into order and gave the enemie such a vollie of shott upon theyre chardge, that they first wheeled, and much discouraged by the death of the Earle of Northampton and Captaine Middleton, with dyvers others gentlemen and officers, they all presently fledd."

Northampton had been unhorsed in this second charge and his charger killed under him by Gell's salvo. Clarendon now takes up the story.

The Earl of Northampton, the Royalist commander killed at Hopton Heath

From the author's collection

> "He (Northampton) was left encompassed with his Enemies. What his behaviour was afterwards, and their carriage towards him, can only be known by the testimony of the rebels, who confessed, that after he was on his feet he killed with his own hand the Colonel of Foote who made first haste to him; and that after his head-piece was stricken off with the but end of a Musket, they offered him quarter; which, they say, he refused, answering 'that he scorned to take quarter from such base rogues and Rebels as they were'. After which he was slain by a blow with a Halbert on the hinder part of his head, receiving, at the same time, another deep wound in his face."[4]

But the Earl's death did no more than give temporary respite to the hard-pressed Parliamentarians. The Moorlanders had run away at the second charge, and the death of their leader infuriated the Royalists, who charged Gell's foot again led by the impetuous Byron. Unfortunately, he omitted properly to re-form his troops and attacked prematurely with only part of his force. Gell's musketeers, reinforced by the timely arrival of Brereton's 200 foot under Captain Bowyer, who had just arrived on the field, drove the Royalists off with relative ease, and Byron himself received a disabling musket shot in the thigh. The disorganised Royalists contemplated another attack, but reluctantly decided against it and encamped for the night below the ridge.[5]

Gell's troops, no doubt exhausted by the strain of their first major action, were in due course rejoined by Brereton's defeated troopers, but they were not in any condition to renew the battle. In any event, night had fallen, and too weakened now to attempt an attack on Stafford, Brereton and Gell decided on retreat. During the night Brereton returned with his forces to Nantwich while Gell made a sullen withdrawal through Uttoxeter to Derby, taking with him the stark and naked body of Northampton as a grim trophy of the action. While recuperating his troops at Uttoxeter, Gell received a messenger from Northampton's son asking for the body to be returned. Gell was not a man to give something for nothing, and the emissary received a swift retort – young Compton could have his father's body "if hee would send him the drakes which they had gotten from their dragoones and pay the chiurgeons for embalming it (the body)". Needless to say, this proposal produced no response from the Royalists, and a disappointed Gell returned with the body to Derby where it was paraded round the streets and interred in the Cavendish family vaults at All Saints Church. This barbarous action, which Clarendon describes as "unheard of and against the Law of Arms" earned Gell the enmity of the King who, within days, issued a proclamation excepting him from the amnesty which had been extended to the Parliamentarian supporters in Derbyshire.

Tactically the battle was a defeat for the Parliamentarians. They had suffered about 200 killed and taken prisoner, and perhaps the same number wounded, although they lost no officers of note. In addition the Royalists had captured most of their artillery, and in their haste to leave the battlefield they had abandoned their baggage and ammunition. They had also failed to take Stafford, which was the primary objective of the manoeuvring which had led to the battle. The Royalists, on the other hand, had been left in command of the field, retained Stafford, received a welcome addition to their train of artillery and sustained only some 50 casualties. They had, however, lost Northampton, and had two captains killed, whilst Byron and the Earl's son were both wounded. Strategically, however, the encounter made little difference. Although Prince Rupert took Lichfield Close from the Parliamentarian garrison a month later, it presented no immediate threat to Derby and once on home ground again Gell was able quickly to bring his forces up to strength again. In effect the Royalists, distracted as they were by the pressing demands of other theatres of war, were unable to exploit their victory, and Gell was left relatively unmolested to consolidate his position in the county.

5 Gell triumphant

Major Mollanus.....broke thorrow the enemy and brought in the dragoones and entred the towne again and drove the enemy before them, many of them slayne, and one hundred and sixty taken prisoners, but one man of our side slayne.
Sir John Gell on capturing Nottingham.

On 8th April 1643, Colonel Lewis Chadwick, of Mavesyn-Ridware in Staffordshire, a commander of horse in the army of the Earl of Essex, sent word to Gell that the eccentric Lord Deincourt, having evidently overcome his attack of parsimony when approached to lend money to the King, was not only sending assistance to the Royalist garrison at Bolsover Castle, but had fortified his own home Sutton Scarsdale, about three miles from Chesterfield. Gell, at that time desperately short of funds, had been busy levying forced loans (a euphemistic description for extortion) on Royalist supporters in the county, including Deincourt who had "contributed" £80. Perhaps this persuaded him to throw in his lot with the King; whatever the reason, his presence between Derby and Chesterfield was a clear threat to communications and a worrying pressure on Gell's rear area; furthermore, Deincourt's position in the north of the county might well stir-up the inactive Royalists in the High Peak, and plainly he would have to be removed without delay. Chadwick informed Gell that he had already gathered some three hundred horse from Scarsdale and South Yorkshire, and Gell immediately reinforced them with five hundred men and two guns, led by his brother Thomas and Major Molanus. The size of Deincourt's garrison is unknown, but it must have been fairly substantial for, Gresley tells us, it "obstinately held out for a long tyme". Ultimately, however, the besiegers were successful, taking the house, Deincourt and all his men prisoners for a loss of two or three of their own men. Such light casualties suggest that the attack on Sutton was largely an affair of trenches and bombardment, and that Thomas Gell, no match for his brother in aggressive spirit, held back from a full-scale assault. Deincourt was put on parole to surrender himself at Derby within eight days, and the Greycoats demolished the earthworks around the house and returned home; not surprisingly, Deincourt broke his word and speedily placed himself under the protection of the Royalist garrison at Newark, where he occupied his family's property at the Friary. Gell's reaction to his brother's lenient treatment of Deincourt is unrecorded, but can be imagined; although Thomas Gell continued to take an active part in military operations from time to time, he justified his appellation of "Sweet Tom Gell" in the doubtless more congenial atmosphere of the Derby Committee. Gresley

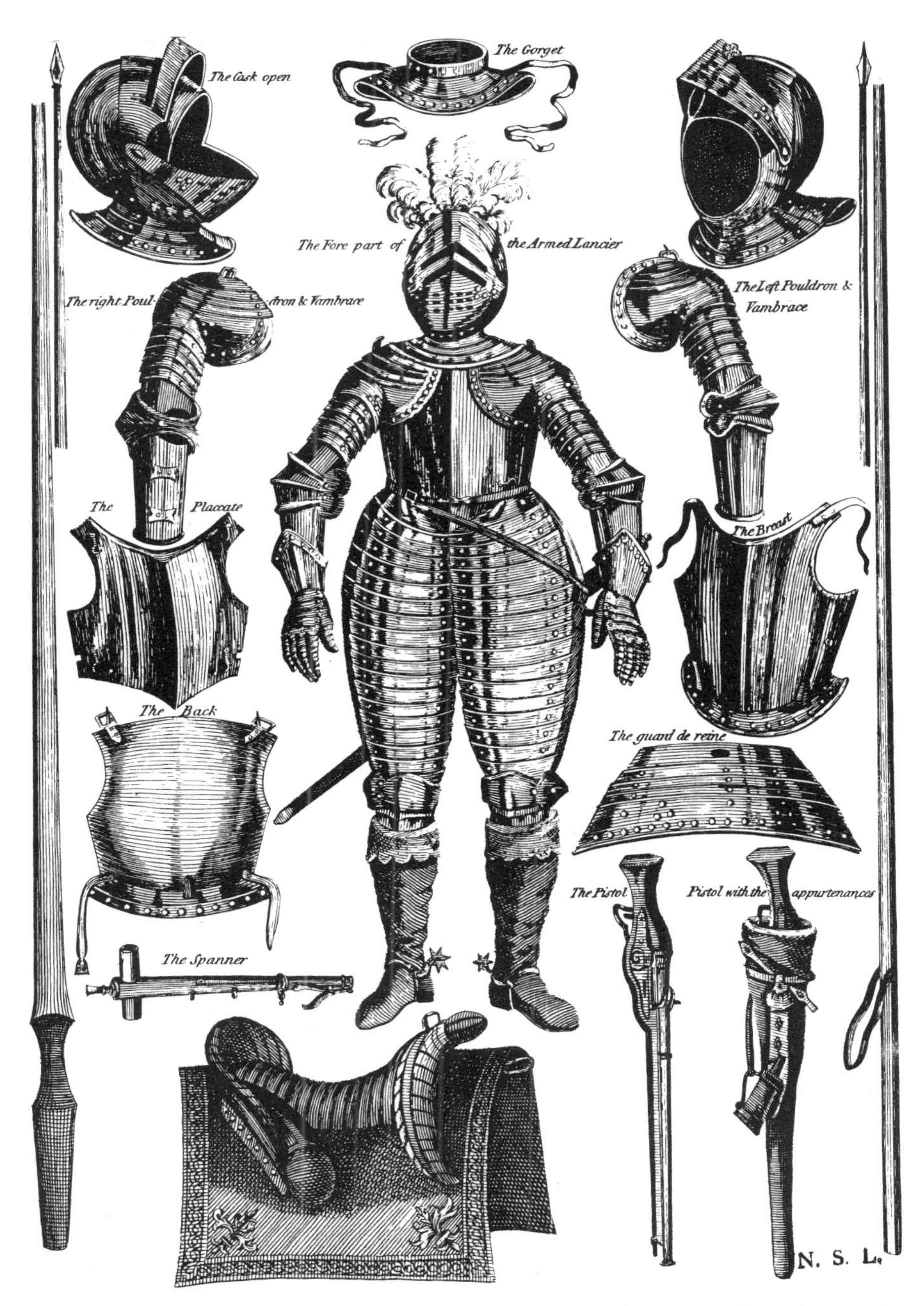

Horseman's armour. Full armour like this was usually kept for ceremonial occasions, only the breastplate and backplate being worn in battle

From the author's collection

was forthright in his comments:

> "...that Lord, contrary to the articles, went early the next morning to Newarke, which perfidious dealing of his, our very adversaries have since, in some measure, revenged, for the garrison at Bolsover pillaged the house, and those of Newarke caused hym to unburye his money and to bestow it in the maintenance against God and the Kingdome; his lands the cavaliers have leased, because they know not how to take it, which cannot be better bestowed than towards the discharge of publique engagements; and so then that lumpe of fleshe will bee neither for service of Kinge or Parliament."

Prince Rupert, meantime, was approaching perilously close to Derby. Storming Birmingham on his way and slaughtering the defenders, he invested Gell's garrison at Lichfield Close on 10th April. After a siege of 11 days he sprang a mine under the defenders and took the Close, the first time that such a device had been used in England. It was clear that Derby was his next objective and the garrison, under their Chief Engineer, Edward Lion, worked feverishly to repair and improve the fortifications. "We mended our workes", says Gresley, "and called in other garrisons expectinge our own turne next". But the Prince, hastily recalled by the King to counter the Earl of Essex in the Thames Valley, was unable to exploit his position, and leaving a garrison in Burton he returned with his forces to Oxford. Gell again demonstrated his resilience; notwithstanding their less than cordial relations since the abortive attack on Ashby, within days he had sent to Lord Grey of Grobey for assistance in retaking Burton, whose garrison he had withdrawn to reinforce his troops at Derby; two days later their force united on Egginton Heath, and Burton was attacked and the Royalist forces driven off. Gell garrisoned it with a company of foot some 200 strong under Captain Sanders and a gun, and shortly reinforced it with sixty dragoons, thus securing the vital river passage over the Trent and Dove.

In the adjoining county of Nottingham, meanwhile, the position of the Parliamentarians had become extremely grave. Not only were they threatened by the large and active garrison of Newark, under the leadership of their new governor, Sir Richard Byron, but the Earl of Newcastle had thrown a garrison into his house at Welbeck, and the Earl of Chesterfield's house at Shelford Manor in the Vale of Belvoir had also been occupied by a strong force led by his son Philip. The garrison of Bolsover, which had been established in February by Newcastle, continued to carry out depredations in the north-west of the county, and north Derbyshire, and indeed, in the words of Mrs Hutchinson "...Nottingham thus beleaguered with enemies, seemed very unlikely to be able either to resist the enemy or support itself". This caused serious concern in London. By late April the House of Commons was writing to Sir Thomas Fairfax of Yorkshire that he should "be pleased to afford them what aid you in your great wisdom shall think fit for the relief of their very pressing and urgent necessities". This worrying situation was compounded by two ominous developments. In Yorkshire, Newcastle's capture of Wakefield had freed him to concentrate his army on overwhelming the garrisons of Rotherham and Sheffield; in addition Queen Henrietta Maria had landed at Bridlington in February, and, under a hail of shot from the Parliamentarian fleet, unloaded 13 transport ships filled with arms and munitions for the King's army at Oxford. She had been at York since 7th March, seeking a favourable opportunity of joining her husband, and her obvious route was through the North Midland counties of Nottinghamshire and Derbyshire.

The nearest forces available to counter Newcastle's threat to Sheffield were a detachment of Gell's Greycoats at Chesterfield under his brother Thomas. Although these numbered only about 250 men with two small field pieces, "being earnestly importuned by Sheffield men, and others, to joyne with them and some promised forces from the Lord Fairfax", Thomas Gell moved his men north to the assistance of the Sheffield garrison, which they had worked so hard in January to establish. On his way, however, he had the good fortune to fall in with two of his own men who had been assisting the garrison of Rotherham when it was attacked and taken by Newcastle on 7th May. Joining Newcastle's army they took their opportunity to escape, and informed Gell that the town had fallen and that Sheffield Castle had been abandoned by its garrison. Lacking the promised help from Fairfax, then engaged in an attack on Wakefield, Gell had no option but to retreat to Derby, leaving the way open for Newcastle who, from his new base at Sheffield "miserably plunders and takes all before hym, leavies great summies of money, and raiseth more men by the commission of aray; we were again threatened, and expected daylie to be besieged" (Says Gresley) "and ... we were never more in danger than at that instant". At this critical juncture, Gell called for assistance from Captain Sanders at Burton, whose men were badly needed to reinforce the Derby garrison. To his chagrin, however, he discovered that Sanders had been seduced from his allegiance by the local Parliamentarian Commander in Burton, one Colonel Haughton ("a Lancashire man"), who had appointed Sanders his Lieutenant-Colonel, and availed himself of the services of his troops. "He refused", says Gresley in exasperation, "in this our extremity to come unto us, yet he sent us his coulours and commission but kept our men armes and horses". Gell was never to forget this untimely disloyalty, and although Sanders later returned to the service of the Derbyshire Committee, their relations were permanently scarred by the incident; indeed, this personal feud, as Gell now saw it, culminated in bitter political fighting during the so-called "Recruiter" elections of 1645.

Fortunately for Gell, Newcastle's threatened invasion of the county never materialised. Hearing of the capture of Wakefield by the Fairfaxes, he pulled his army back into Yorkshire. No sooner had one threat disappeared,

A dragoon, or mounted foot-soldier. According to the military textbooks he fought on foot, using his horse only for greater mobility

From the author's collection

however, than it was replaced by another. On 4th June the Queen set out from York with 4,500 men intent upon reaching the King in Oxford. Within days she was at Newark, by now one of the strongest and best fortified Royalist garrisons in the country. Parliament was well aware of the Queen's likely intentions, and at the end of May they ordered all available Midland Association forces to join Lord Grey of Grobey at Nottingham to succour the endangered garrison there and to prevent a junction between the Queen and King. Leaving his brother and one foot company to garrison Derby, Gell marched with the rest of his regiment and most of the ordnance to the rendezvous bringing Grey's strength up to about 5,000 men, "most of them horse". This was probably the biggest force that the Parliamentarians had yet managed to muster in the area. As well as Gell with perhaps 800 men, Grey was joined by his own Leicestershire forces, Colonel Hutchinson's and Pierrepoint's Nottingham Regiments, and a strong force from the Eastern Association led by Oliver Cromwell. "Then", says Gell sourly, "(we) marched upp and downe in the Vale of Belvoir for the space of one moneth". This comment somewhat underrates what was actually done by the Parliamentarian forces, but it is hard not to feel some sympathy for Gell, for much more could have been achieved given decisive leadership. Unfortunately, this was the one factor that was lacking. The Derby men were placed under the command of Lieutenant-General Hotham, whose attachment to the Parliamentarian cause was already on the wane. Within a few months, he and his father had attempted to betray the Parliamentarian garrison at Hull, and they were both arrested and later executed. Gell and Grey, as we know, disliked each other, and Cromwell was so beset by financial problems that he could not pay his troops and had to borrow £100 from the Nottingham Corporation. Grey's forces were supposed to march into Yorkshire in order to assist the Fairfaxes and pre-empt the Queen's march to Newark, but Hotham, whether out of disloyalty or indecision, objected. Lingering at Nottingham, uncertain what to do, Grey decided to attack the outlying Royalist garrison at Wiverton House in the Vale of Belvoir, and sent his whole force there including Gell's Greycoats. After attacking the outworks and beating the enemy into the Manor House, Grey inexplicably withdrew. But in a day or so he returned and recommenced operations. Mrs Hutchinson describes what happened.

> "(They) planted their cannon against it within pistol shot and were resolved to lie there that night, but news was brought that all Newcastle's force was marched out with – (sic) Newark, which news, though Major Ireton told my Lord that it would be a deed of great dishonour to him to retreat, and that they were there to fight with them if they should care, yet they all drew off and returned to Nottingham.".[1]

"And then", she continues,

> "was Nottingham more sadly distressed by their friends than their enemies; for Hotham's and Gell's men did not only lay upon free quarter, as all the rest did, but made such a havoc of friend and foe, that it was a sad thing for anyone that had a generous heart to behold it."

The arrival of the Queen at Newark on 16th June finally decided the Parliamentary Commanders that their proposed march into Yorkshire would have to be abandoned; on 21st June, some of the Queen's troops attacked the Parliamentary forces, killing 50 and taking 80 prisoners, but it must have been clear to the Queen that Nottingham was too strongly reinforced to attempt to force her way through it. Ironically, the Parliamentary Commanders had decided by now that they were too deficient in foot to prevent the Queen from marching to Oxford, and accordingly says Gell "my Lord Grey retreated towards Leicester, Cromwell towards Peterborough, Colonel Hubbard with his regiment tarried at Nottingham, under the command of Sir John Meldrum, and Colonel Gell to Derby". The unreliable Hotham was arrested by Colonel Hutchinson and Cromwell, and the Parliamentary forces broke up in disarray having achieved nothing. This humiliating demonstration of the inability of the local Parliamentary forces to act effectively in concert, must have given pause for thought to the House of Commons; although the lesson was slow to be learned, it gradually became apparent that Parliament could only defeat the King if it could match his main field army with an even more disciplined and centrally controlled army of their own, hence the formation of the New Model Army in April 1645.

On his return to Derby, Gell must have been slightly consoled to learn that his depleted forces in the town had achieved a modest victory in his absence. While Gell was manoeuvring aimlessly in the Vale of Belvoir, word came to his brother that Sir Richard Fleetwood had fortified his house at Wootton Lodge in Staffordshire from where he was able to intercept and capture the carriers that went weekly from London to Manchester via Derby and the Cheshire/Lancashire border. The Lieutenant-Colonel, accompanied by Captains Swetnam and Mellor and their companies, numbering about 400 men, and a troop of horse, attacked the house, took it by storm and returned to Derby with Fleetwood and his garrison of 80 as prisoners. Gresley describes Wootton Lodge as "one of the strongest places in that county, exceeding well provided of all necessaries and manned with such a company of obstinate papists, and resolute theeves, as the like were hardly to be found in the whole Kingdome". This minor success, however, scarcely compensated Gell for the position in which he now found himself. The Queen, failing in her attempt to force Nottingham, marched through the Vale of Belvoir to Ashby, where she was

A fully-equipped musketeer, with sword for hand-to-hand fighting, though the musket itself, held by the barrel, made an effective club

From the author's collection

joined by the tireless Hastings. This placed Gell's garrison at Burton in the gravest jeopardy; in an attempt to retrieve the situation and forestall the Queen's attack, he sent into Staffordshire for reinforcements and despatched a messenger to Nottingham, which was still heavily garrisoned by Meldrum's men, seeking immediate assistance. Drawing his men out to the appointed rendezvous at Eggington Heath, he waited in vain for Meldrum's men and the Staffordshire Parliamentarians to join him; after three days he had no option but to retreat to Derby, and on 2nd July the Queen's forces, led by Charles Cavendish, stormed and took Burton, killing many of the defenders, and taking the rest prisoner, including Lt. Col. Sanders, his new Major of Foot Nathaniel Barton, and Colonel Haughton. By 13th July she was reunited with the King at Oxford, bringing a valuable reinforcement of men and munitions including six cannons[2], two mortars and a large quantity of ammunition. Such was the price of the Parliamentarians' failure to oppose her march to Newark and Nottingham.

Gell promptly sought an opportunity to redeem the position; receiving intelligence that Hastings was at Tutbury Castle where his forces had

Tutbury Castle, held by Henry Hastings for the Royalists

Photo: D.J. Mitchell

"devoured all the provision they had", he determined to attempt a siege. Appealing once again to Meldrum for help, which he this time received, he marched his entire regiment, accompanied by Meldrum's 200 horse and dragoons, to besiege Hastings in his lair. By this time the Derbyshire forces had received some badly needed replacements for their much used weapons, including "twenty barrells of powder, three hundred muskets, sixty carbines, and sixty cases of pystolls, being the free gyft of the honourable House of Commons". The capture of Tutbury Castle would serve a dual purpose by removing a considerable threat to Derby, while at the same time releasing Sanders, Haughton and their men who had been sent prisoners there after the capture of Burton. Surrounding the Castle, Gell's men entrenched themselves and settled down to starve out the beleaguered Royalists. Within two days, however, Major Ireton who commanded the Nottingham horse returned with his troops, apparently because of a piece of false intelligence that Newcastle was on his way to relieve Tutbury. Without sufficient cavalry effectively to blockade the Castle and to cut off enemy convoys and reinforcements, Gell once again retreated wearily to Derby. Shortly afterwards Sanders was exchanged and returned to Derby to serve as Major in Gell's newly raised Regiment of Horse, but this was to prove an uneasy alliance.

The news of Newcastle's approach to Tutbury was not wholly without foundation, for his army was indeed on the move south, but towards Lincolnshire rather than Derbyshire. Meldrum was ordered to join Cromwell at Peterborough for the relief of the garrison at Gainsborough, and at the beginning of July he left Nottingham in a parlous state; the town was by now surrounded with extensive earthworks which, says Mrs Hutchinson, "would have required at least 3,000 men to man and defend well". The Governor, Colonel Hutchinson, had only 400 men and 14 guns, and had to face the probability that Newcastle would detach a part of his army to take the town from its meagre force of defenders. As so often before, he sent to Gell, his nearest neighbour, for assistance, which he speedily provided in the shape of Major Molanus and three hundred dragoons. These occupied the town whilst it was evacuated, and the defenders moved their belongings into the castle. This must have been a heaven-sent opportunity for the light-fingered Greycoats who no doubt returned to Derby somewhat more heavily-laden than they had left. They were also accompanied by fifteen rebellious Nottingham burgesses and other Royalist sympathizers, including Alderman Drury, who were committed for safe-keeping to Derby Gaol. It was not long before Hutchinson's worst fears were realized; by 18th September Nottingham was occupied by a force of 600 men from Newark led by the redoubtable Sir Richard Byron. They invested the castle closely and proceeded to open a brisk cannonade from the site of St Nicholas Church. The desperate Hutchinson sent at once to Derby and Leicester for help, and Gell again responded readily; Molanus was despatched yet again to Nottingham with 500 mounted musketeers and reinforced with three troops of horse from Leicester. Their arrival caused consternation among the Royalists who began to fall back through the town – Gell relates the incident thus:

> "The enemy was then at least five or six hundred in Nottingham town, horse and ffoot, and stood all in battalio in the market place, and all our fforces were not five hundred. The said Major Mollanus with Captayne Hacker ... entred the towne with their horse, were presently beaten backe, lost four or five horses, instantly after the said Major broke thorrow the enemy and brought in the dragoones and entred the towne again and drove the enemy before them, many of them slayne, and one hundred and sixty taken prisoners, but one man of our side slayne, which was namely one Captayne Leiftennant Lenerick, who led Colonel Gell's owne troope, three men wounded, and some five or six horses killed. Wee relieved at the same tyme at least four hundred townsmen and souldyers of the castle, who were almost famished. The remainder of the enemy fled to Nottingham bridge (Trent Bridge), which they were then fortefying."

Mrs Hutchinson, however, gives a rather different view of the relief.

> "As soon as they were come into the town, Sir John Gell's men, seeing the cavaliers had a mind to be gone, interrupted them not, but being as dexterous at plunder as at fight, they presently went to Toplady's house, who had betrayed the town, and plundered it and some others, while the governor's soldiers were busy in clearing the town of the enemy. When they had done this, the governor did what he could to restrain the plunder; but the truth is, Gell's men were nimble youths at that work ..."[3]

The following day Hutchinson tried to persuade the Derby men to assault the fortified bridge over the Trent, held by Colonel Rowland Hacker and 80 men, "but", Mrs Hutchinson says scathingly "The major of Derby, (Molanus) an old dull-headed Dutchman, said ten thousand men could not do it, and could by no means be entreated to go on, nor to stay one day longer". So the "dull headed old Dutchman" and his men rode back to Derby, where Mrs Hutchinson alleges that they told Gell they could not assault the bridge because the governor refused to lend them a piece of ordnance from the castle. Whatever the truth of the matter, some ten days later, Gell's men returned again to Nottingham at the request of Colonel Hutchinson who had made preparations to assault the fort and bridge, entrenching his men within musket shot of it, and planting ordnance ready for the attack. The failure of the Derby troops to assault the bridge while the Royalists were still in disarray rankled with Hutchinson, while the domineering Gell would not allow that there had been any failure on the part of his forces that might reflect adversely on him. Relations between the two men were obviously strained at this time, and Hutchinson sent a mocking note to Gell "to tell him, if he be pleased to send any of his men, they might come and see the fort taken". The irascible Gell doubtless viewed this tactless message as a personal affront and Molanus was sent back with his men to redeem himself and his Commander's honour. The two accounts of what followed, Gell's and Mrs Hutchinson's, are so contradictory that they cannot be reconciled; it must be remembered that both had strong reasons for putting the best construction on their actions, and the truth probably lies somewhere between them. At all events, Molanus and his men (three or four hundred horse and dragoons says Gell, six score according to Mrs Hutchinson) evidently took part with the Nottingham regiments in the attack on the fort, driving their trenches through the meadows, breaking down a sluice gate erected by the Royalists and draining off the water which had surrounded a small island close to the bridge. Within a day or two they had pushed forward a small party of men on to what was now dry land, "within carbine shot of the bridge", and were ready to attack. But the fort was silent; the Royalists, breaking down part of the bridge behind them, had fled during the night back to the safety of Newark, and so the Greycoats returned home again.[4]

For the first time in his narrative, one can detect a note of uncertainty in Gell "(we) drove the enemy away" he says "so that it will be adgudged by any councell of warr that Nottingham towne and castle had beene long since in the enemy's possession, had they not had the assistance of Sir John Gell ... as the Colonells and Committee of Nottinghamshire did ever acknowledge," a comment that would have been unnecessary if they had indeed acknowledged it. Altogether one is left with the feeling that his Major's caution had caused Gell no little embarrassment. And the matter did not rest there. When it was Gell's turn to face the fury of the Royalist army, he was to find Hutchinson less than openhanded in his assistance. That time was fast-approaching for Newcastle, driven back from Lincolnshire by the efforts of Fairfax and Cromwell, but with Yorkshire secured behind him, was free to turn his attention to an invasion of Derbyshire, the greatest menace yet faced by the county in the war, and one that could well prove the downfall of the Parliamentarian cause in the North Midlands.

6 Newcastle's invasion

During the time of my Lord's stay at Chesterfield in Derbyshire, he ordered some part of his army to march before a strong house and garrison of the enemy's called Wingfield Manor, which in a short time they took by storm.
The Duchess of Newcastle.

Now the focus moves to the northern part of the county. "Receiving intelligence that the enemy was got into Derbyshire and did grow numerous there, and busy in seducing the people, that county being under my Lord's command, he resolved to direct his march thither in the beginning of November 1643, to suppress their further growth". Thus the Duchess of Newcastle, describing her husband's intentions in the early winter of 1643. For many months Newcastle's forces had been hovering around the northern borders of the county, where, assisted by the Royalists of the High Peak, they posed a constant threat to Gell's rear. The garrison at Bolsover, the only Royalist garrison at the time within the county boundaries, caused such concern to Gell and the County Committee that they had had to deplete their own slender forces in Derby to oppose the threat. By early 1643 there were detachments of Greycoats holding all the places of strategic significance in Northern Derbyshire, including garrisons at Wingerworth, the home of the Royalist Sir Henry Hunloke, Chatsworth, recently abandoned by the Cavendish family, and Wingfield Manor. After the taking of Sutton Hall from Lord Deincourt, it also was occupied, as was Renishaw Hall and Staveley. Newcastle's abortive invasion in May had resulted in the occupation of Chesterfield for some ten days, during which time the Royalists had a brief encounter with Gell's men and attempted, unsuccessfully, to take Wingfield Manor. By the late summer of 1643, Wingfield was held by no less than a company of Gell's modest forces under Lieutenant John Todd, an officer in Thomas Gell's company of musketeers; the dispersal of Gell's forces throughout the county was exacerbated by the demands of Fairfax; in the late autumn of 1643 Fairfax was in Nottingham with two thousand horse seeking reinforcements for a projected march into Yorkshire. Gell went to see him at Nottingham and Fairfax suggested an approach to John Milward, whose house was at Wingfield, in the hope that he could be persuaded to take up arms for the Parliament. Milward had held a commission as a Captain in the Derbyshire Trained Bands and was evidently considered to be a man of some influence in the county and therefore a valuable recruit. The accounts are confusing, but it seems that Gell had previously sent emissaries into the Peak to see Milward and other possible Parliamentary supporters, but without much

Snitterton Hall, home of Colonel John Milward

Photo: D.J. Mitchell

success. Milward, however, had already committed himself to the King, and by early 1644 was busily engaged in raising a regiment of Dragoons, so these various approaches came to naught. Gell then invited Fairfax to Derby, where he was asked to assist in another attempt on Tutbury Castle. His response was unhelpful; not only did he refuse but requested Gell to let him have four or five hundred musketeers to assist his march to Chesterfield and hence into Yorkshire. Gell must have been at his wit's end, for his scattered forces were scarcely able to defend Derby, let alone deal with the threat of a resurgent Newcastle. However, by dint of further depleting his garrisons in North Derbyshire he was able to provide Fairfax with some 250 men, 60 from Wingfield's garrison of 100, the same from Captain Taylor's company at Wingerworth, 40 men from the Chatsworth garrison and most of Captain Hadfield's company.

The rendezvous was appointed at Chesterfield for the following Saturday and Nathaniel Hallowes and Thomas Gell, in their capacity as members of the County Committee, rode there with all haste to make arrangements for the provision and quartering of Fairfax's men: that same evening they were joined by the detachments from Wingfield and Wingerworth, but by now Newcastle had already begun his move into Derbyshire. The following day his advance troops were no more than two miles from Chesterfield; Fairfax consulted with his Commanders, decided upon a retreat south and left the Derbyshire forces, as Gell says "to shift for themselves". Hallowes and Gell quickly withdrew the remnants of their troops from Wingerworth and Chatsworth and returned to Derby. Chesterfield was occupied by Newcastle's troops and Derbyshire was about to face the most critical period of the war.

The Duchess of Newcastle's version of the invasion is laconic in the extreme.

> "During the time of my Lord's stay at Chesterfield in Derbyshire, he ordered some part of his army to march before a strong house and garrison of the enemy's called Wingfield Manor, which in a short time they took by storm. And when my Lord had raised in that County as many forces, horse and foot, as were supposed to be sufficient to preserve it from the fury of the enemy, he armed them, and constituted an honourable person (Hastings) Commander in Chief of all the forces of that county and Leicestershire; and so leaving it in that condition, marched, in December 1643, from Chesterfield to Bolsover in the same county, and from thence to Welbeck in Nottinghamshire...in which parts he stayed some time, both to refresh his army and to settle and reform some disorders he found there, leaving no visible enemy behind him in Derbyshire, save only an inconsiderable party in the towne of Derby, which they had fortified, not worth the labour to reduce it."[1]

All this rather gives an impression that Newcastle met with little or no opposition in his march into Derbyshire, but this was not so; late November and early December of 1643 probably saw some of the severest and most protracted fighting yet witnessed in the county.

As soon as he had occupied Chesterfield, Newcastle decided to attack Wingfield Manor before its tiny garrison could be relieved or withdrawn. On 15 December Sir Francis Mackworth settled down before the Manor with 500 horse and dragoons and some field pieces, outnumbering the defenders by ten to one. At that time the Manor was still in a reasonable state of repair, "strengthened" says a Royalist newsletter:

> "by a strong embattled wall of fifteen foot high and ten foot thick. The rebels refused to yield it up upon summons, whereupon Sir Francis played upon it with his cannon but (through the great strength of the wall) did not much harm to the house. At length, upon exchange of the body of a gentleman slain by the King's forces for one killed near the walls who could not be brought off, some words passed, when Sir Francis told them, that if yet they would surrender they might find favour, which offer was soon embraced: and after a short treaty they were allowed to march away, leaving all their arms behind them, being about 160, with good store of ammunition and above three months provision, all of which was taken in

Some of the stages in loading and firing a matchlock musket. It took a trained soldier several minutes to load and fire this type of gun.

From the author's collection

> the house, which through its strength and situation, standing in the middle way between Derby and Chestefield, will be very advantageous to His Majesty's affairs."[2]

Doubtless Gell was grateful that his little garrison had come safely home, for he needed every available man to oppose Newcastle's advance in the north and west and Hasting's approach in the south. But his position was still extremely grave; on 19th November, Royalist agents from Bolsover had entered Derby and endeavoured to raise a riot during which they could seize the county magazine. They were discovered and driven off losing one of their number killed; Gell's troops were beginning to desert and he had to place a heavy guard on St Mary's Bridge and lookouts on the tower of All Saints. In addition he was desperately short of gunpowder, sending to Hutchinson for a supply of ten barrels, he met with an understandable refusal; Hutchinson's position at that time can scarcely have allowed him to lend the Derby Committee so substantial a proportion of the gunpowder that he needed for the defence of Nottingham. The Derby Committee men, no doubt under considerable strain, were exceedingly annoyed:

> "he told them they should have four barrels, but they in a great chafe at it, flung out of the room...Yet the next day returning they were something more calm and came and desired five barrels, which the governor...allowed to them, but Sir John Gell was very angry they had not their full demand."[3]

Gell's personal attention must have been fully occupied during this crisis, provisioning the town, strengthening the earthen bastions, supervising his train of 28 pieces of artillery, and writing numerous letters for support to the Commons, Fairfax, and anyone who would lend an ear. But his combative temperament would not allow him to remain wholly on the defensive. Sanders was desptached to South Wingfield where, in a skirmish with Sir John Fitzherberts' Regiment, he took two Captains and forty soldiers prisoner. A few days later he had another encounter with forward elements of Newcastle's army at Kilburn, where he worsted them again coming off with one Major Wheeler and 90 men prisoners, and all their horses and colours; one of the colours is described and is typical of the religious and allegorical subject matter of many civil war standards "a man paynted and standing with a goold axe under a greene tree, with this motto: rout and branch". The man with the axe doubtless represented the King cutting down the tree of rebellion, and the motto is evidently an ironic reference to the "Root and Branch" bill for the abolition of episcopacy that had been supported with such enthusiasm by the puritan members of the Long Parliament.

Molanus was not inactive either. As Newcastle's troops pushed forward from Bakewell towards Hartington and the Staffordshire border at the end of November, Gell despatched him to Leek to assist the Moorlanders with

350 horse and dragoons. But the Earl's forces reached them first and cut them to ribbons; a Royalist newsletter gives a gleeful account of the action.

> "Colonel Dudley...went towards the enemy's quarters about Hartington towards Staffordshire, with an intention to beat up those quarters; but not coming so soon as to perform that intention, the rebels drew out a body of two thousand horse and foot (such as they were) and with a hideous noise, proclaimed the expectation they had of a sudden victory. But it pleased God otherwise to dispose of them; for Colonel Dudley (leaving only a good reserve of foot and one troop of horse) charged the rebels with all the rest of his horse and foot in a full body at once, which was so home, that with his horse he beat quite through their rear of foot into the midst of their horse, and forced them to a disorderly retreat; and not willing to give them time to recollect, he pursued and slew above one hundred of them upon the place, following the chase into Staffordshire near five miles together (almost to Leek) and doing sharp execution all the way. Then he drew up his horse in order, and made a stand, and sent back a messenger to know the success of the foot, who had by that time routed all the rebel's foot, only three hundred or thereabouts retreated into the church which they had prepared with strong baragadoes, but before this messenger came thither, the foot had forced one of the church doors, and taken and slain every man of them. They took ten officers, three colours of foot, and one of horse, and among others the brother of Colonel Ashenhurst."[4]

The "brother of Colonel Ashenhurst" here referred to was Randle Ashenhurst of Glossop, who had been a Captain in Gell's own troop of horse; in about mid-November, he had deserted Gell's service with his troop of 40 horse and put himself, like Sanders, into the service of the Staffordshire Committee, his brother being one of the local Commanders.

Had Molanus known of Ashenhurst's presence among the defeated Moorlanders, he would doubtless have viewed it as being no more than poetic justice; as it was, his late arrival on the scene, unsupported by the defeated Staffordshire men, left him impotent to do anything other than cover his own retreat to Leek after a sharp skirmish in which he killed five of the enemy's officers and took thirty-six prisoners. There he tarried for a fortnight, waiting for support from the Staffordshire Committee, which never came, and in mid-December returned to Derby, taking prisoner 26 of Newcastle's men at Ashbourne on the way.

So far the honours had gone to the Royalists. The action at Hartington forced the evacuation of Gell's last remaining stronghold in North Derbyshire, the garrison under Captain Stafford retreating to the support of the Derby garrison, while the Royalists "pillaged to the gates of Derby". If Newcastle had taken this opportunity to attack Gell's headquarters, it is highly probable that he would have overcome the weakened and dispirited garrison, and the Parliamentary cause in Derbyshire would have been lost or at least severely retarded; but Newcastle was no strategist. He was a

Cavalry arms drill. Pistols and carabines were always the newer and more expensive flintlocks

From the author's collection

charming, accomplished and very wealthy aristocrat with no military training, and a penchant for theatre. Ben Johnson's Masques "Love's Welcome at Welbeck" and "Love's Welcome at Bolsover" were written specifically for Newcastle, who was his patron, for the entertainment of King Charles on his way north to be crowned in Scotland. At 51, his natural caution had also been crystallized by his age and he was distracted by ominous events to his far rear, on the Scottish border.

For many months the English Parliamentarians had been in negotiations with the Scots, whose differences with the King were, if anything, even more intractable; so far, however, they had held aloof from the war. On 23 September Parliament had accepted the Solemn League and Covenant with the Scots, whereby they undertook to impose a Presbyterian form of Church Government in England similar to that enjoyed by the Kirk in Scotland. Three months later they had successfully concluded an alliance and the Scots began to prepare an army to invade England, twenty thousand men paid and equipped at the expense of Parliament. On 19th January 1644 they began to cross the Tweed, and Newcastle's forces on the border fell back to Berwick. Newcastle had no option but to abandon the occupation of Derbyshire and any hope that he might have had of uniting his forces with the King's, and at the end of January he was already marching north to face the Scots Army; what the Royalists had dreaded most, a war on two fronts, had come to pass, and Derbyshire had been saved by the Scots.

Newcastle's presence in the northern hundreds, however, had undoubtedly encouraged the Royalist party there, and given them much needed leadership and material assistance, and Gell was to spend much of the succeeding year in containing and reducing the resurgent Royalists. "He leaves to vex us" says Gresley "his own garison at Bolsover, and six Collonells of his owne country, whereof five, namely Sir John Fytsherbert, Sir John Harpur, Mr Fretchvile, Mr Ayre and Mr Milward, had such regiments as theire own interest, backed with the commision of array, and the popeishe party, could raise for them". During his stay at Chesterfield, Newcastle had managed to raise no less than 2,300 recruits for the King, and considerable sums of money; and Gell had to face a considerably strengthened garrison at Wingfield which had been repaired and improved and was occupied by Fitzherbert's Regiment under the governorship of Colonel Roger Molyneux of Hasland Hall. In the south, too, the ever present Hastings had seized the opportunity offered by Gell's weakness to reinforce his garrison at Wilne Ferry, one of the three vital crossings of the Trent, and had fortified Kingsmill, and in the west, Sir John Harpur had entrenched himself at Burton Bridge. Gell would have his work cut out to restore the balance, and he wasted no time in making a start.

7 Gell resurgent

Our horse, coming neare the enemy, and hearing that Colonell Eyre, his regiment, lay in Boylston church, our dragoones dismounted, and surprised the whole regiment in the church; and soe took men, armes, collours, and all without loss of one man on either side.
Sir John Gell.

Even before Newcastle had withdrawn his army northwards, Gell was in action again. On 6th January 1644, Molanus, with several hundred horse and dragoons, fell upon Harpur at Burton before he had had time to complete his fortifications. There was a sharp encounter in which five Royalists were killed at the mouth of the Bridge towards Derby, and most of the rest were captured. The Parliamentarians returned to Derby with five hundred prisoners, including Harpur's Major, six Captains and eight other officers, but the elusive Harpur made good his escape. And so, says Gresley with some satisfaction, "the whole regiment was spoyled". Molanus suffered no fatal casualties and had only a small number wounded.

A month later, shortly after Newcastle's departure, Gell himself decided upon an attack at Kingsmill, recently fortified by Hastings, to support his entrenchments at Wilne Ferry. Mrs Hutchinson's Note Book gives a detailed description of the incident.

> "the horse went with Sir John Gell to Kings Millnes, hard by Wilden Ferry, where there is a very strong house, wherein the enemy kept garrison, against which Sir John Gell had planted his ordnance on the other side of the river, where his foot also were, but his horse and ours were all on the same side the house stood. The weather being very tempestuous, they resolved to finish it at once, and thereupon drew out five men out of every troop to begin the assault, these five of every troop made thirty in all; they had attempted, but fruitlessley, to fire the house, so these thirty men in the night got over their works, and slided down the bank, which was very steep, till they came just under the walls, which when they within the house perceived they called for a parley, and desired to march out with bag and baggage, but the soldiers would grant them no conditions but to yield to their mercy, so when they were just about to open the door by force, the soldiers within the house let them in and yielded themselves, there being in the house forty-seven, a captain, a lieutenant, and two more officers."[1]

Meanwhile, the forces left behind by Newcastle in the north of the county were proving a considerable irritation. Royalist troops from Bakewell and Tissington met daily at Ashbourne to intercept trade in the area and to provision their own men at the expense of the local farmers, whose produce was seized on its way to market. Sanders was sent with five hundred horse and dragoons to help them and to assist the Staffordshire Moorlanders in the siege of Biddle House which Hastings was threatening to relieve. Having news of his approach and intending to attack and beat up his quarters in Ashbourne, they drew together three hundred horse and foot and approached secretly hoping to take him unawares. Gell relates what followed.

> "Our men having intelligence that the enemy was approaching, drew all our dragoons into the lanes and hedges, and charged them: and our horse falling on the reare of them, routed them all and pursued them to the towne of Tissington, and took one hundred and seventy prisoners, and many of them slayne."

This severe mauling forced the withdrawal of the Royalists from Bakewell and Tissington and they fell back on their garrisons at Stanley, Chatsworth and Wingfield.

Whilst Gell pursued his vigorous counter-attack in the county, the Parliamentarians were at last taking decisive action against the Royalist garrison at Newark which had been a constant menace to Nottingham for the past twenty months. On 24th February, Gell was ordered to send all his horse and dragoons to aid Meldrum in blockading the stronghold. With reinforcements from Grey at Leicester, and Rossiter in Lincolnshire, Meldrum managed to concentrate about 5,000 men, and on 29 February he closely invested the garrison; within a few days the besiegers were at close quarters with the Royalists, and after a brisk action had taken the Spittle to the south west of the town. In order to protect his rear, Meldrum also took and fortified the Muskham bridge over the northern arm of the Trent, which leaves the main flow of the river to the west of Newark in a looping curve and rejoins it some 2 or 3 miles downstream. The pioneers engaged on this vital work were protected by Gell's Derbyshire horse under Molanus while his dragoons were thrown into the Spittle from which they galled the enemy with artillery and small arms fire. These developments around the King's most important garrison caused considerable anxiety at Oxford and Prince Rupert was despatched with a force of 6,000 men to raise the siege. By 21st March he was at Bingham, and early in the morning of that day there was a savage encounter between the opposing armies' cavalry in which the Parliamentarians lost over 200 killed and were forced into precipitate retreat over Muskham bridge, leaving a large force cut-off and surrounded in the Spittle, incluing most of Gell's dragoons. Rupert and Meldrum negotiated terms of surrender by which the Parliamentarians were to deliver up the Spittle with all their firearms and were permitted to walk away "with colours flying, swords and pikes, the horsemen with their

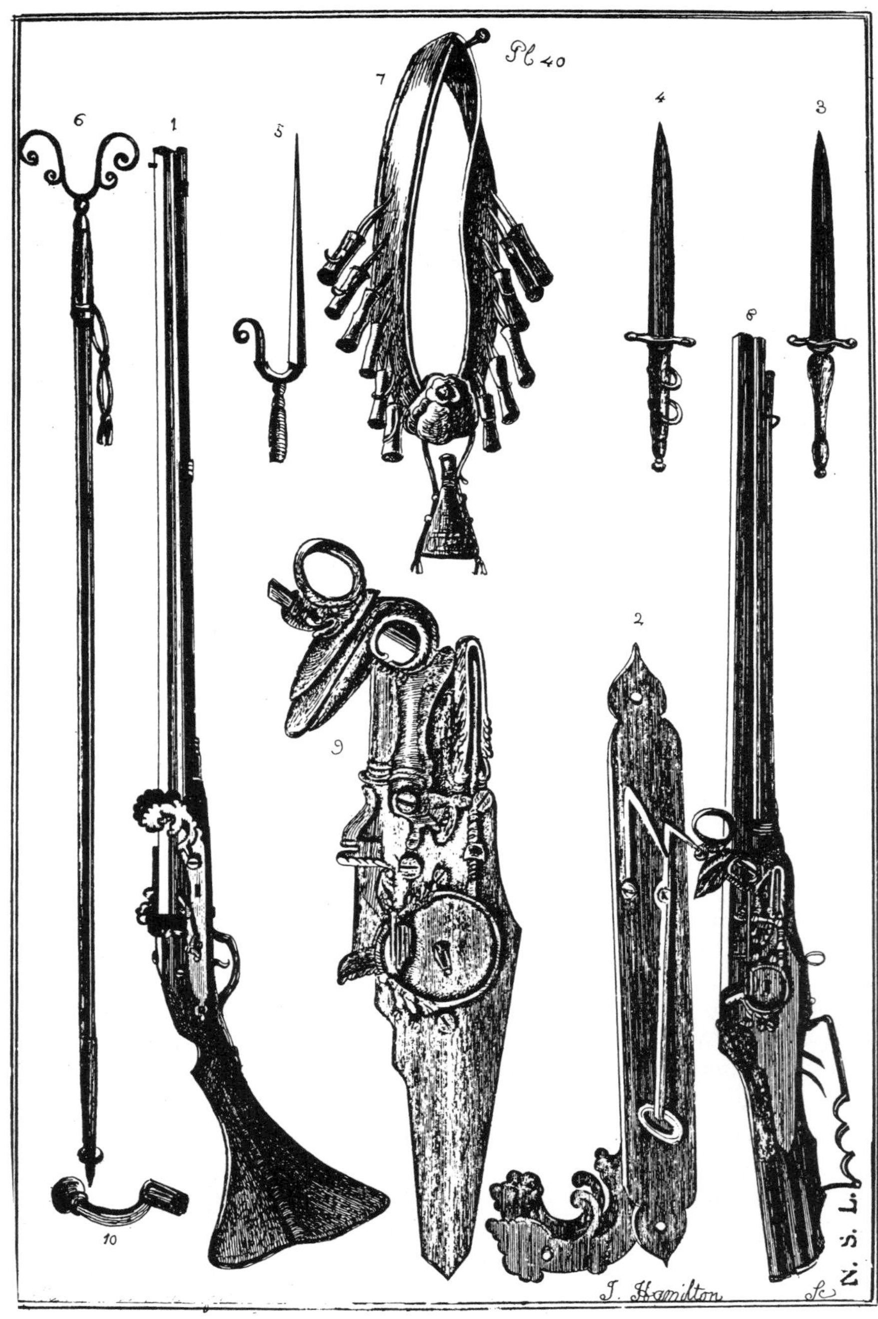

Details of firearms, including the flintlock mechanism and some early plug bayonets

From the author's collection

horses and swords and all the commanders with their pistols".[2] But the Prince's men, remembering the ill treatment of their comrades at the taking of Lincoln, broke the articles of surrender and, comments Gell with asperity "the men (were) all stript to their very skin". In this disaster, for such it was, Gell lost more than two hundred horse and dragoons, with all their arms and ammunition, a severe reverse which must have retarded his attempts to settle affairs in the north of the county.

Having raised the siege, Rupert again returned to Oxford, pausing on his march at Ashby where his troops and Hastings took the opportunity of plundering the surrounding countryside. Gell took immediate steps to prevent them.

> "He presently sent all his horse out towards Egginton Heath, Captayne Rhoades being chief commander thereof. As soon as they came to the heath, the enemy appeared above six hundred strong, and ours but about three hundred and fifty; whereuppon, Colonel Gell having intelligence of the enemy's strength, sent presently Major Mollanus out with four hundred ffoot, towards Eggington Heath, to lye in the lanes wayting, least his horse should bee forced to retreate, that they might be ready to fall uppon the enemy if they should pursue them; but before the ffott came neare them, our horse most valiantly had routed them, and driven them into Trent river, where many were drowned and slayne, and two hundred taken prisoners."

Some 250 years later, a sad relic of this skirmish was uncovered on the heath, in the form of a Royalist cavalry sword.[3]

Notwithstanding the relief of Newark, the Royalists in the north were now everywhere on the defensive; the Scots army had pressed Newcastle's forces back into York and Parliament was able to look to the re-supply of its hard-pressed forces in the Midlands. At the beginning of April 1644 Gell received news that forty guns were being sent from London to Peterborough for him, and he made arrangements to convey them to Derby. In many respects this must have been one of the most hazardous operations of his career; the road from Peterborough passed perilously near to the Newark garrison, and at Ashby Hasting's forces posed a constant menace. Heavy guns, such as these were, could only be moved at an agonizingly slow pace of about 5 miles per day, and they would be an easy target for Royalist cavalry and dragoons. Gell sent Molanus with 100 horse and dragoons to Lord Grey at Leicester, seeking his help if it should prove necessary. Grey had heard that strong Royalist forces were converging on Tamworth from Bridgnorth, Dudley and Lichfield and he and Molanus joined forces and marched there in order to frustrate the enemy's plans. This having been achieved, Molanus and his men went to Peterborough to convoy the train of artillery, while Grey sent scouts to Newark in order to protect the convoy's right flank on its return march. The safe arrival of the guns at Derby must have been a considerable encouragement to Gell, who could now utilize some of them in subduing the Royalists at Wingfield.

Throughout the spring and early summer of 1644 this energetic little garrison had forayed and plundered unceasingly in the Scarsdale Hundred, and appeared undismayed by the defeat of the Royalists at Ashbourne. It was supported by the presence of Newcastle's troops at Bolsover and clashes were frequent. "It is impossible to relate" says Gresley, "our continuall and almost daylie incounters with the Earl of Newcastle's garrisons at Bolsover and Welbeck" and the perceptive comment of Mercurius Aulicus, that the possession of Wingfield would be greatly to the King's advantage, was adequately supported by events. Operations against the Manor began in early June, when the whole of Gell's regiments, except two companies left in Derby, beleaguered the garrison, assisted by Colonel Thornaugh from Nottingham with some troops of Horse. For ten days they entrenched themselves outside the walls and were shortly reinforced by a body of 200 foot, also from Nottingham. Evidently, however, these early attempts met with little success. Wingfield, as Newcastle's siege in December had demonstrated, was an extremely powerful stronghold, and the Royalists had had plenty of time to strengthen the massive earthen bulwarks, the remnants of which can still be seen today on the northern side of the building.

Wingfield Manor, besieged by both sides in turn

Photo: D.J. Mitchell

In the north, however, great events were shaping which were to speed the fall of Wingfield to the Parliamentarian forces. 22nd April 1644 found Newcastle besieged in York by the combined armies of the Scots and Fairfax who were to be joined on 3rd June by Manchester's army of the Eastern Association, some 30,000 men in all. It is beyond the scope of this book to detail all the movements that led to the great and decisive battle of Marston Moor, but we must digress briefly to discuss it so that later events in Derbyshire and the downfall of the Royalist cause there can be understood. Prince Rupert was sent by forced marches to assist Newcastle, carrying a letter from his uncle the King, which was in part to prove his undoing. "If York be lost" wrote the King, "I shall esteem my crown little less...but if York be relieved and you beat the rebel's army of both kingdoms which are before it, then...I may possibly make a shift to spin out time until you come to assist me".

On his march north the Prince detoured through Cheshire and Lancashire in order to relieve Lathom House and near Bolton he was joined by a large detachment of Newcastle's forces under Goring. On 1st June, Gell had written to the Committee of both Kingdoms concerning the movement of the Royalists around Sheffield.

> "Our country Colonels Fretchwell, Eyre and Millward, with their chief force of horse and foot, after several marches to Sheffield and back again with their carriages and most of their strength, on Thursday and yesterday marched after Goring; they have quitted Chatsworth, the Earl of Devonshire's house, but they still keep the rest of their garrisons in this county; Fretchwell took along with him eight colours of horse, averaging about 20 to a colour, but his foot were not many; the other Colonels had about 100 horse, 30 dragoons and 220 foot. These are all gone into Cheshire, pretending to join with Prince Rupert and to raise the siege of York."[4]

Rupert reached York on 1st July and on his approach the Parliamentarians broke camp and commenced a withdrawal to Tadcaster. The following day, reading the King's letter as positive instructions to attack and defeat the greatly superior Parliamentarian armies, Rupert and Newcastle deployed for battle on the bleak uplands of Hessaye Moor, later known as Marston.

The Derbyshire Royalist horse was placed on the right and centre of the left wing where Eyre and Freschville commanded some 400 men under Goring. Milward's body of 220 foot were to the left of the second line in the centre, and to their right was probably the regiment of another Derbyshire Royalist, John Shallcross of Shallcross who had joined Newcastle in York some time previously. The battle opened with an attack by the Parliamentarian left wing under Cromwell on the Royalist right led by Rupert and Byron, whose men were soon in retreat. Goring on the left wing, however, was equally successful against Fairfax's Parliamentarian horse, and the lines of battle pivoted clockwise on the field, locked together and fighting furiously. But the Parliamentarians, who were more disciplined than the Royalists, eventually reformed more quickly, and after three hours of bitter fighting they won the battle and the remnants of Rupert's army trailed back to York. And it was indeed a remnant, more than 3,500 Royalists had been killed, 1,500 taken prisoner and many wounded, and the Parliamentarians had also suffered severely, losing perhaps as many as a thousand. The Derbyshire Royalists, both horse and foot must have been decimated; Freschville, Eyre, Milward and Shallcross all escaped to fight another day, but Shallcross's Royalists in particular must have been virtually wiped out, fighting as it was with Newcastle's Whitecoats who, scorning quarter, were cut down to a man. Altogether this thundery summer day in Yorkshire witnessed one of the greatest battles ever to be fought on English soil, nearly 40,000 men of both armies engaged in probably the most decisive engagement of the Civil War, resulting in the destruction of the Royalist fortunes in the North.[5]

Boyleston Church, where Gell's men captured an entire regiment of Royalists

Photo: D.J. Mitchell

The serious defeat had immediate repercussions in Derbyshire, where the garrison at Wingfield could no longer expect aid, but they held on grimly. Gell had been diverted from his attack on the Manor by the activities of Hastings, who was gathering together a relief force for the Royalist detachments at Lichfield, Tutbury and Ashby, forcing Gell to detach Sanders with all his horse and dragoons to meet him; it was here that Rowland Eyre, recently arrived from his defeat at Marston Moor, his troops no doubt weary and dispirted, had the misfortune to be captured. Gell gives a vivid account of the incident.

> "Our horse, coming neare the enemy, and hearing that Colonell Eyre, his regiment, lay in Boylston church, our dragoones dismounted, and surprised the whole regiment in the church: and soe took men, armes, collours, and all without loss of one man on either side."

These 200 or so men were left in the church under guard of a strong party of dragoons, while Sanders marched the rest rapidly to Burton where Colonel Bagot and a force of Royalists from Lichfield had just entered the town. Sanders then

> "assaulted the enemy; and after two or three hott encounters, beatte them cleare out of the towne, where there were five of our side slayne, and seventeen of the enemy, and many of them taken prisoners, and brought back to Boylston church to the other prisoners, which made upp three hundred in all: and soe marched with them to Derby, with six ffoott collours and one horse collour, with all their armes; and soe our men and horse returned to the leaguer at Wingfield Mannor againe."

But Gell's ordnance was insufficient to the task, and by now the siege must have been absorbing on increasing proportion of his time, men and resources. The defenders were tenacious in their defence of the Manor; earlier in the siege Gell's men had cut the pipes of the underground water supply, but Molyneux sank a well in one of the courtyards and drew up rules for its use; the soldiers of the garrison were given priority, and after them the horses and the garrison's solitary cow. "To women" continued Molyneux's order "none, but by the order of my hand". Each of the 34 horses was allowed 1½ gallons per day, and among their owners besieged in the garrison were the Catholic Major Thomas Eyre (brother of Rowland) who would later negotiate terms with the besiegers, and the last Commander of the Garrison, Colonel Danby. Molyneux sent letter after letter to Hastings for assistance, many of which were intercepted by Gell. In one of them dated 30th July he informs Hastings that he has already been besieged for 9 days and that the enemy's cannon were "trenched very close, bombasting the tower where the well was and firing canies" (canister).[6] At length, Gell despairing of the effect of his own guns sent to Major-General

Crawford at nearby Sheffield for help,

> "finding that his ordnance would do noe good against the Mannor, and understanding that Major Generall Crawford had foure great peeces, sent two of his officers unto him, to desire him to send him them for three or foure days for battering: and in soe doinge hee would doe the countrey good service, because it was a place that could not be otherwise taken, without they were pined (starved) out."

Crawford came in person, accompanied by his guns, demi-cannon firing a 32 lb shot, and some horse and foot, and they were entrenched on the highest point of Pentrich Common on the site of the old Roman Camp at Coney Green. This is a good 1,200 yards from Wingfield Manor, and although the bombardment caused the Royalists to evacuate a half-moon battery[7] on the south-east side of their works, the range was too great to effect a breach. Even the heavy demi-cannon had only an extreme range of 1,700 yards, and to batter the earth-reinforced walls of the manor they would need to be much nearer to their point-blank range of 400 yards. So on 14th August Gell and Crawford moved them to the west side of the Manor and from the edge of the wood at Wingfield Park Gate they opened a heavy fire on the walls. After three hours, a breach had been opened, the defenders called for a parley, and Wingfield was surrendered. The Royalists, some 220, were allowed to march to their own homes; Gell captured 12 guns, 250 muskets and 150 pikes. In the confusion, the governor, Danby, disguised himself as a common soldier and endeavoured to escape, but he was recognized by a deserter who thrust his musket through a loophole in the porter's lodge and shot him in the face, killing him instantly. So ended the longest and most testing siege of the war. At a conservative estimate, at least some of Gell's forces had been continously engaged in it for some ten weeks, and the relief in Derby at the surrender of the garrison must have been very great. Gell left a detachment of two full companies of foot and a troop of horse to ensure that this vital position was adequately held to meet any further attempt on it by the Royalists.

Having disposed of this substantial drain on his resources, Gell was able to turn his attention to an equally great menace nearer at hand, the garrison at Tutbury Castle. This, together with the Royalist outposts at Ashby and Lichfield, were a focus for the defeated Royalists from Marston Moor, many of which fled to these various garrisons after their defeat in July, where they were able to reinforce Hasting's troops and, as Gell said "began to robb and plunder in Derbyshire and Leicestershire". To prevent this, in early October, Gell established a blocking garrison at Barton Hall, about three miles from Tutbury, under the governorship of Captains Nathaniel Barton and Robert Greenwood, from which he could harry the defenders of Tutbury, attack their convoys and cut off stragglers. In 1645, according to the Royalist Richard Symonds, it had a garrison of 700 horse, but it is likely that the forces were smaller than this initially.[8] Encouraged by the success of his venture, Gell also assisted the Leicestershire County Committee in setting up a similar blocking force at Coleorton, about two miles from Ashby, which he assisted throughout November with his entire force of horse and dragoons not otherwise engaged. In November of 1644, Thomas Gell and Gresley were writing of their achievements to the Earl of Essex, in an attempt to persuade him to permit the establishment of a permanent garrison at Burton.

> "We have settled a garrison at Barton Parke, in this County, within two miles of Tutburie, which so curbs that garrison, that on Thursday last, the soldyers there laid down theyre arms and refused to serve any longer without present money."

Gell ended the year on a high note: on 5 December he had reinforced Colonel Rossiter, the Parliamentary Commander in Lincolnshire with six troops of horse; while patrolling in the Vale of Belvoir they encountered a large force of Royalists under the governor of Newark, Sir Richard Bryon, and, says Gell,

> "charged and routed them, slew many of them, and drove many of them into a brooke, that they were drowned: and Sir Richard Byron,...had much a doe to save himself, in running on ffoott to Belvoyer Castle, leaving his perriwicke behind him on the ground, many of them taken prisoners and our troopes brought with them about thirty good horse to Derby, which made some satisfaction for oure losse before Newarke."

This literally hair's breadth escape for Byron doubtless caused some amusement to the Parliamentarians; whether they had the courtesy to return the Governor's wig, however, history does not record.

8 Gell in retreat

Wee sent severall lettres to Sir Thomas Fayrfax, ernestly desiring his ayd, wee had only promises but no assistance. In the meane tyme the enimy pillaged very near Derby, and our neighbour countrymen...returned home.
Sir George Gresley.

Thus far, our story has been dominated by Sir John Gell, and certainly during the period from the opening of the war to early 1645, his personal position in the county and his single-minded and purposeful prosecution of the war was virtually unchallenged. But in the country at large, a gradual shift of political power was taking place that was paralleled in Derbyshire by the rise of Gell's greatest rival, Major Thomas Sanders.

Sanders was born in 1610, and was the owner of a modest estate at Little Ireton. Educated at Derby School and Repton, he did not attend university, and at the outbreak of war in November 1642 he obtained a Commission as a Captain of Foot in Gell's Regiment. He appears to have been typical of the lesser county gentry of the period; unlike Gell, however, who in spite of his dubious morality was a strict Presbyterian, Sanders' religious views inclined more towards Independency, and as such mirrored the increasing power of the Independent faction in Parliament, and particularly the army.

It is difficult for us in the twentieth century to appreciate the fundamental and overwhelming importance of religious belief to the seventeenth century man, who devoted himself to his own particular brand of faith with a single-minded tenacity rivalled, in our day, only by the dogmatism of the Marxist or the fanaticism of the Nazi. Indeed post war analysis of seventeenth century English history has grossly underplayed the importance of this aspect of the life of the ordinary man in determining his motives and his actions. We have already seen how, in Derbyshire, one of the crucial factors affecting the choice of sides in the Civil War was religious inclination, and certainly Presbyterians, by and large, tended to support Parliament. The effect of two years of war was, if anything, to polarise both political and religious views, and by late 1644 there is no doubt that Independency was a force to be reckoned with both in the capital and the counties. Precisely what was an Independent, however, is not so easy to define. Broadly, however, the differences amounted to this: Presbyterians believed that there should be a "national" form of church government, based roughly upon the organization of the Scottish Kirk, i.e. a unified countrywide adherence to one mode of religious worship, governed not by Bishops, but by a series of "classis" or convocations of elders from each congregation, with, at the apex, a national convention or synod to conduct and order the affairs of the church. Independents, on the other hand, were more akin to what we now call "Congregationalists". They did not believe in a national form of Church government, but rather in the liberty for each congregation to conduct its own affairs with its Ministers in the way it decided best. In the event, the Independents' "liberty of conscience" was not in fact extended to other beliefs, such as Quakerism, but such is the nature of religious belief, today as in the seventeenth century! If this distinction, that was to have such profound effects during the Interregnum, seems to us so artificial as to be incomprehensible, that merely illustrates how far removed we are in habits of thought from our forbears of three hundred years ago, because it was, without doubt, a matter of prime political importance.

Hand in hand with the Independents' radicalism in religion went a certain radicalism in politics, so that, by early 1645, the Parliament had effectively split into two parties: the Presbyterians, finding their Scots brethren uneasy bedfellows, and distrusting the increasingly vociferous Independents, under Cromwell, moved further and further towards a policy of negotiating terms with the King. The Independents, however, seeing their own position threatened by such a compromise, and disliking the theocratic notions of their Parliamentary opponents, became the party of unconditional surrender; thus differing religious views tended also to distinguish rival political ones. This division was exacerbated towards the end of 1644 by the formation of the New Model Army.

It had been clear to Parliament for some time that their combination of three main field armies, that of the Earl of Essex in the Thames Valley and Home Counties, the Earl of Manchester's Army of the Eastern Association and Sir William Waller's in the West, were unlikely to reduce the King's armies to impotence unless they were placed unequivocally under one command, centrally organized and directed. Time after time the efforts of these forces, and the Parliamentary militia in the counties, had been nullified by dissension between local commanders, each intent on his own parochial concerns. In Derbyshire, as we have seen, Gell's priorities were usually local ones, and the threat of a Royalist descent on the county would usually result in his troops being hastily recalled from whatever joint operation they were then engaged upon. This disunity of command scarcely made for a vigorous prosecution of the war, and it hampered the development of a coherent strategy for the defeat of the King. On 23rd November 1644, therefore, the House of Commons ordered the Committee of Both Kingdoms to "Consider of a frame or model of the whole militia". By 6th January 1645, the Committee had placed before the House proposals for the establishment of one main Field Army, the "New Model", to consist of 22,000 men; 6,000 horse, 14,500 foot and 1,000 dragoons, made up of the Earl of Essex' army, the Earl of Manchester's

Eastern Association Army, which included Cromwell's famous Ironsides, and the shattered remnants of Waller's army, defeated at Roundway Down and Lansdown. They also proposed a "Self-Denying Ordinance" whereby members of the Parliament, whether commoners or Peers, were to be excluded from any command in the new army; plainly this was an attempt to reduce the influence of the Presbyterian "peace party" over the operations of the New Model, or at least so it was perceived, and the House of Commons rejected the proposal. By the time it was eventually passed on 3 April, Cromwell had managed to get himself excluded from its provisions, and had become Lieutenant-General with Sir Thomas Fairfax in command.

Of course, this division between peace and war parties, Presbyterians and Independents, should not be viewed in rigid terms. For one thing, the New Model did not incorporate all the Parliamentarian forces; there were still independent armies operating in the north and west, and the Scots Army, some of whom were now quartered in Derbyshire and South Yorkshire, fell wholly outside the control of the English Parliament. In the North Midlands too, a strong Parliamentary army under General Poyntz, a veteran of the Thirty Years War (where he fought on both sides), took the brunt of the fighting in 1645, when it distinguished itself by massacring the Royalist garrison at Shelford House, in the Vale of Belvoir. Furthermore, at least some Presbyterians continued in their allegiance to the Commons; Colonel Hutchinson, for instance, in neighbouring Nottinghamshire, continued in his unwavering opposition to the King, and was one of the signatories of the King's Death Warrant. Fairfax also remained a committed, and moderate, Presbyterian, notwithstanding his command of the New Model.

These developments, however, which greatly increased the extra-Parliamentary power of the Independents, must have fuelled the flames of Gell's already bitter feud with Sanders, and it did nothing to improve his relationship with Fairfax, of whom Gresley had commented in the autumn of 1643

> "wee sent severall lettres to Sir Thomas Fayrfax, ernestly desiring his ayd, wee had only promises but no assistance. In the meane tyme the enimy pillaged very neare Derby, and our neighbour countrymen, dispayring of any ayd from Sir Thomas Fayrfax, returned home..."

Gell's disagreements with Sanders had started as far back as May of 1643 when, it will be remembered, he deserted the service of the Derbyshire Committee and placed himself and his company at the disposal of the Staffordshire Parliamentarians, who gave him a Commission as a Colonel. Gell was not the man to forget disloyalty, and although Sanders was subsequently released from captivity after his capture at Burton, and returned to Derby again, the breach between the two men was already too deep to be healed. Their differing views on the prosecution of the war, particularly after 1646, were compounded by their personal differences, and Gell took every opportunity to do down his rival.

In October 1643, Sanders had become a member of the County Committee, until then largely controlled by Gell and his supporters, four of the members indeed were related to him by blood or marriage, namely his step-brother John Curzon, one of the MPs for the County, his brother Thomas, and his sons-in-law John Wigley and Henry Wigfall. Sanders' appointment, however, placed as it were, an enemy in the camp, and although he had little support at first within the Committee, he rapidly increased his influence outside it. Hitherto Gell's troops of horse were confined to those raised by his friend and fellow Presbyterian, Sir George Gresley. Sanders, however, was able to raise a considerable number of horse, and to appoint his friends, mostly like-minded Independents, to serve as officers under him. In December 1643, we find Gell writing a most unusually humble letter to Sanders.

> "I am contented you shall have full power and authority to constitute and appoint captains and all the inferior officers belonging to a regiment of horse according to the agreement formerly made betwixt us...I only desire to except my own troop."[1]

This must have hurt Gell's vanity considerably, and the division between the two men widened irreparably when the time came, in November 1644, to elect a new Recorder for Derby to replace the Royalist Allestree. His brother Thomas, already the family lawyer and a member of Gray's Inn, was Gell's natural choice, but he had soon to face the opposition of Sanders, who wrote to his friend and supporter Exuperius Fletcher from the garrison at Coleorton that Thomas Gell was

> "unfit for the place...in respect of his mean estate, want of learning, law and honesty, his conversation being so scandalous, for unclean swearing and hating all honest men; that he favoured malignants and enemies in arms and was not to be trusted or confided in."[2]

These remarks, predictably, infuriated Gell who descended on the next meeting of burgesses at the Town Hall and upbraided the absent Sanders; but Sanders was a man of some moral courage and was not intimidated. His speedy response to Gell, in the form of a letter, shows just how much, by now, they were at daggers drawn.

> "I wonder at your slanderous words spoke of me in the open hall at Derby...I desire my actions and yours to be compared and weighed as I hope before long they will be. I think the Lieutenant Colonel an unfit man to be Recorder and I will hinder it all I can and show reason for it. For two

> brothers and two sons-in-law solely to rule a county, all honest men resent. What I said to manifest his unfitness I will not deny. I seek not the place of governor or colonel."[3]

But these rivalries, bitter as they were, had to be suspended, for although early 1645 saw less military activity than hitherto, the war was not yet finished. In April of 1645, Gell's horse, presumably under Sanders, had returned from Chester where they had been sent to the assistance of Sir William Brereton, then engaged on the siege of the city. They were therefore available to assist the forces of Nottinghamshire in response to a request from a harassed Colonel Hutchinson, in whose absence in London a strong force from Newark had seized the Trent Bridge. No sooner had they been forced to relinquish their hold on it, however, than the King in person began to move towards Derbyshire with his remaining field army out of Oxford. In the far north, the Royalist Presbyterian Montrose had scored a number of spectacular victories over the Scots army, and the King, in a last despairing throw, was hoping to join up with him and inflict a crushing defeat in detail on the New Model and the Scots Army in England. By the beginning of May he was at Tutbury and the Derby garrison worked feverishly on the town defences and awaited an attack. Prince Rupert, in a piece of pure German medievalism summoned his astrologers to predict the outcome of his assault.[4] Fortunately for Derby, however, their prognostications were gloomy; in addition, an attack on Leicester seemed more likely to draw Fairfax and the New Model away from the King's Capital at Oxford where they had entrenched themselves for a siege. On 29th May Leicester was stormed, sacked and many of the garrison massacred and within a day or two, the King persuaded by Rupert that he should reverse his march and relieve Oxford, was on his way south towards the field of Naseby.[5]

On 14th June 1645, the New Model had its first real trial of strength when it faced the King's Army at Naseby. The outcome was not in serious doubt. The Parliamentary army outnumbered the King's depleted forces by nearly two to one, and although the veteran Royalist foot in the centre had an early success against the new recruits of the Parliamentary army, the formidable discipline of Cromwell and Ireton's horse saved the day. As evening fell, 1,000 Royalist dead littered the battlefield, and some 5,000 prisoners marched into captivity. The King's last throw had failed. Gell's part in all this is obscure, but what appears to have happened is this. He had been asked to assist the new Model under Fairfax with his horse and foot. Here is his version of events:

> "There came a letter from the Committee of Both Kingdoms to Colonel Gell, that hee should draw to Nottingham with his horse and dragoons, where they had commanded all the horse and dragoons of Cheshire, Staffordshire, Nottinghamshire, and others to meet at the rendezvous at

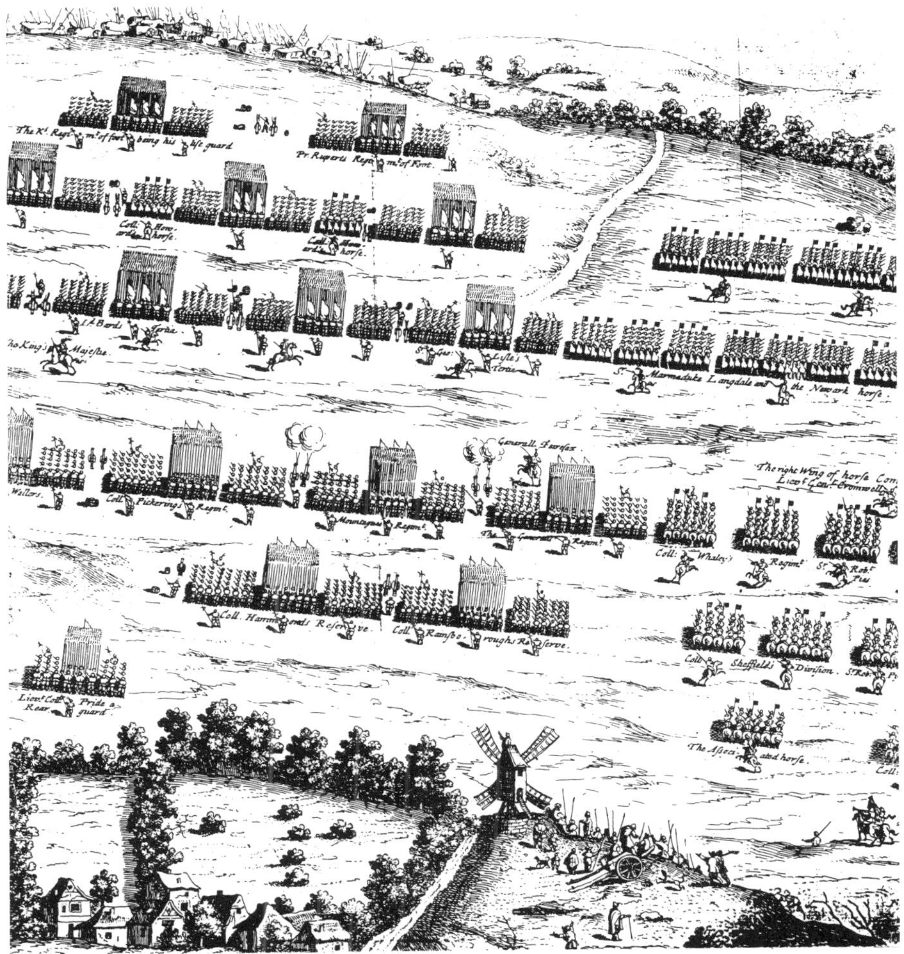

Part of an engraving showing in conventional form the armies drawn up before the Battle of Naseby

From the author's collection

> Nottingham, under the command of Colonell Gell, and hee, with all the said fforces to follow the Kinge, what way soever he marched. As soon as the fforces came together (which was att least fourteen dayes first) Colonel Gell advanced; in the meane tyme, the Kinge was routed at Naysby, and his excellence, Sir Thomas FFairefax, advancing towards Leicester, commanded Sir John Gell to lye with his fforces on the north side of it, and soe the towne of Leicester was surrendered, and afterwards hee dismissed Colonell Gell, and all the fforces that were under his command."

In truth, Gell did very little, and his lame explanation convinced few. Fairfax's Chaplain, Joshua Sprigge, who wrote a history of the Naseby campaign commented "it was the wonder of all men how they [the king's forces] (being in such a tired and distracted condition) could escape Sir John Gell's horse" and Fairfax, although reluctant to accuse Gell of outright insubordination, was also critical. In a letter written to Gell's enemy Sanders he said...

> "a few days before Naseby Battle the General (Fairfax) sent an express to Sir John Gell, (who then had in a body considerable strength of Derby, Nottingham, Stafford, Cheshire and Yorkshire horse) to come with all speed to join with his army, for that there was likely to be a sudden engagement with the enemy and in that letter there was this expression or to the same effect, "for the Kingdom's sake" to hasten thither...Sir John Gell's forces came not to the General till he was a little off Leicester, being the next or two days after the battle. For his not confronting the King's forces according to order, the General cannot well call to mind that business, more than an unwillingness presented, but of disobedience cannot say, that order being allowed afterwards."

In the light of subsequent events, we may surmise that Gell was less than fully committed by now, to what he saw as the "unconditional surrender" policy of the Independents, in addition, the presence of Sanders and his fellow Independents Gervase Bennett, Swetnam and others on the County Committee had reduced Gell's control over his men, and this was compounded by a shortage of money with which to pay his troops. Shortly after the Naseby battle, Gell was ordered to take his own regiments of horse and dragoons to Coventry to rendezvous with the Nottinghamshire and Staffordshire forces, but he says "when hee had marched as far as Synfen Moore, part of his horse began to mutinie for want of money, and turned back". Certainly Gell tended to keep his horse and dragoons, mostly Sanders' supporters by now, on short commons, but it is at least as likely that their differing views as to the prosecution of the war contributed to this unfortunate episode. For reasons that are still imperfectly understood, Independency was strongest among the horse, and a contemporary observer had commented as early as December 1644:

"Look what a company of Troopers are thrust into other regiments by the head and shoulders, most of them Independents, whom they call godly precious men; nay, indeed, to say the truth, almost all our horse be made of that faction."[6]

For the remainder of the year, however, Gell seems to have recovered some of his former vigour, and his horse and dragoons in particular, were kept busy on "mopping up" operations in Nottinghamshire and the Vale of Belvoir, some of them involving severe fighting. The defeat of the King's last major field army at Naseby left his scattered and broken forces to make shift for themselves as best they could, and many of them joined the Newark garrison from whence they harried the surrounding countryside. On 16th July a strong party took the Parliamentary garrison at Welbeck by suprise, and Colonel Freschville with 250 foot was appointed garrison commander. This brought an immediate call for help from the Commander of the Nottingham horse, Colonel Thornaugh, and Gell marched with all his horse and dragoons to meet with him at Wingfield; he handed them over to Thornaugh and they went forthwith to Welbeck where, he says "they tarried awhile and encountered twice or thrice with the enemy, and

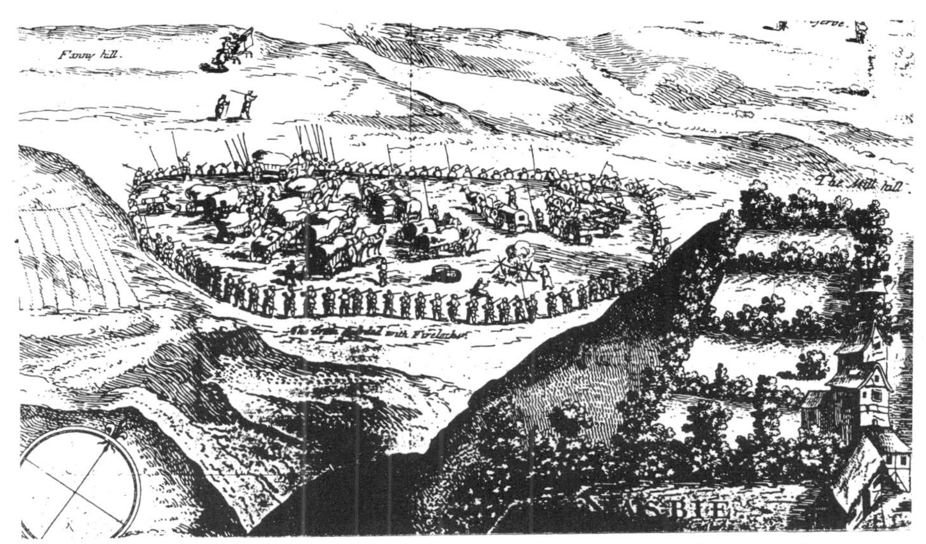

Detail of the Battle of Naseby showing the Parliamentarian baggage train

From the author's collection

beate them, and tooke many prisoners". There were also regular clashes between the Tutbury garrison and Greenwood's men at Barton Blount. The surgeon's bill for the treatment of soldiers wounded in one of these engagements in July 1645, is still extant and is quoted by Firth in his classic *Cromwell's Army*. The approach of the King, however, resulted as usual, in their hasty recall.

For months after the Battle of Naseby, the King wandered up and down the country, endeavouring to recruit his forces. In September he was defeated again at the Battle of Rowton Heath, while trying to relieve Chester, and in an attempt to concentrate his remaining forces into a new army, decided to march to Newark. By the beginning of October he was at Lichfield, and he marched from there to Tutbury with, says Gell,

> "three thousand horse, and from thence to Ashbourne, where our horse fell in the reare of them, and took a Major, much esteemed by the Kinge, and twenty-five prisoners, which major was afterwards exchanged for one Major Gibb, who was Major over the horse in the associated countyes...and soe the Kinge marched through the High Peake to Doncaster."

On 4th October he arrived in Newark, and proceeded to set the disordered affairs of the garrison into a semblance of order.

Shortly before the King's approach, Gell had attempted yet another abortive siege of Tutbury Castle in conjunction with some of the Staffordshire forces, but was unable to pursue his design, having been ordered by the Committee of Both Kingdoms to have 500 foot "ready uppon an hower's warning" to join Col-General Poyntz in a projected siege of Newark. It was perhaps as well that he kept his foot in reserve, for the beginning of October saw another Royalist incursion into the county. Colonel Shallcross ("one of our country Colonels") descended on and garrisoned Chatsworth with 300 horse and dragoons from the Welbeck garrison, freshly augmented with men by the arrival of the King, and Molanus' men who had been sent to Tutbury, were despatched to besiege it. "Having layne their fourteen dayes" says Gell, "and hearing of the demolishing of Welbecke, Bolsover and Tickhill Castles, (Molanus) was commanded by Colonel Gell to return to Derby". This was about 9th November 1645. Shallcross had no doubt heard of Freschville's agreement with Poyntz to disgarrison Welbeck, and totally isolated now from his parent garrison, decided to do the same.

By now Gell's troops must have been exhausted, but they were called upon for one final effort. On 28th October Poyntz at last notified Gell that his men on standby would be required for what was to be the last siege of Newark. First, however, Poyntz had to reduce the outlying garrisons. Shelford, Wiverton and Welbeck had already been stormed or surrendered, which left the Royalist garrison at Belvoir commanded by the formidable

Sir Charles Lucas, later to be executed by Fairfax at the Siege of Colchester. Lucas had reinforced the medieval castle with strong entrenchments and earthworks, and on 17th November Poyntz had encamped at Bottesford and prepared his assault. The defenders, undeterred by the massacre of the Shelford garrison, defended their outworks ferociously. Gell's men were fully employed in the assault, and lost 11 killed and 27 wounded, for which "the Parliament bestowed £40 amongst Derby souldyers to drinke." No doubt they needed it, for the attack on the outworks was successful and Poyntz, taking example from his experiences in the Thirty Years War, was not a man to give quarter to a recalcitrant garrison. Many of the defenders were slain and the rest fled into the Castle which surrendered at the beginning of the following February.[7]

Throughout the winter and spring Molanus's men continued as part of Poyntz's army until the final surrender of Newark on 8th May 1646. It was a notably hard winter, and the Newark garrison maintained their reputation for vigorous activity to the last. Early in the morning of New Year's day 1646, Poyntz's camp at Stoke was attacked by a party of 800 horse and 300 foot. Most of the Parliamentary horse fled from the field, but the Derbyshire foot under Molanus stood firm, and during a fierce three-hour battle lost 4 killed and 30 wounded (including Molanus' own Lieutenant Drinkwater) and had 30 men taken prisoner. The Newarkers eventually retreated, having lost 72 men killed and wounded. Gell comments with satisfaction "Colonel-General Poynts gave them many thanks in the open field, where they stood in battalio, for their courage and valour". In spite of his hesitations at Naseby, Gell could afford to see his role in 1645 with a certain degree of complacency; but the seeds of his downfall had already been sown in one of the most extraordinary political events of the entire war in Derbyshire, the Recruiter Election of November 1645.

9 The Recruiter Election

He that stands for Mr Gell stands for the Devil, for he is a worthless man and a man of no trust. They that give their voice for him do damn themselves and their posterity to the Pit of Hell.
A citizen of Derby.

By the middle of 1645, the membership of the Long Parliament was much reduced by death and by the defection of many Royalist members to the King's Parliament at Oxford. Of the original number of 507, 236 were Royalists, who were disabled from sitting as members, and at least 14 had died, even before the war broke out. It therefore became a matter of urgency to hold elections for the vacant seats, some of which had been unrepresented for two years or more. The waning of the King's cause after the Battle of Naseby, and a return to more settled conditions in many parts of the country, allowed Parliament to begin issuing writs for the elections in August 1645, and thereafter they proceeded apace. These elections, which took place gradually over 1645 and 1646 and even, in some cases, as late as 1648 were known as the "Recruiter Elections", and they gave a focus to the disagreements between the Presbyterian Peace party and the Independent War party in the House.[1]

In Derbyshire there was one seat to be filled, that of the absent Royalist Allestree, who had been Recorder of Derby and one of the two MPs for the Borough with Nathaniel Hallowes; the writ for the election arrived from the Commons on 10th September 1645, and by then the lines of battle were already drawn. Gell proposed his brother Thomas, the new Recorder, while Sanders and his supporters, by now quite powerful on the Committee, supported the candidacy of Robert Mellor, a burgess and Committee Member and Captain in Gell's Regiment of Foot. Gell and Sanders, although sitting on the same Committee, were, by now, hardly on speaking terms. Their bitter feud had continued unabated since the election of Thomas Gell as Recorder. In April of 1644 Gell was declaring, to anyone who cared to listen, that "he had rather fight with Major Sanders than with any Cavalier in England and that he would have his pennyworth out of him", and the clashes between them since had been numerous. By mid 1645 indeed, relations had become so bad that Gell had actually imprisoned one of Sanders' officers, Captain Robert Cotchett[2] of Mickleover, and subsequently banished him and his family from Derby, treating his friend and supporter Captain Barton likewise. Gell's problem was to remove potential Mellor voters from the Borough while the election was held, and in a shrewd ploy he sent Mellor himself and his Company, which included many of his supporters, to garrison Chatsworth, recently evacuated by the Royalists. Not only did this remove at a stroke about 60 of Mellor's voters, but it left Gell's brother, whose Company continued in garrison in Derby, in a strong position. Mellor protested, but Gell threatened him with his cane, and Mellor did not feel able to bring matters to a head with a man who was, after all, his military superior.

With Mellor and many of his supporters gone, Gell then embarked upon a systematic campaign of intimidation against the rest. Two burgesses, Youle and Dunnage were dragooned out of Derby at musket point. Dunnage had the temerity to argue the point unwisely comparing his loyalty, by implication at least, with Gell's. Gell was furious "Sirrah" he shouted, "do you make comparisons?" and he then punched the unfortunate Dunnage in the face making his nose bleed. These unseemly activities continued for some weeks; the term of office of the Mayor, Luke Whittington, who had complained of Gell's hectoring of the burgesses, expired and he was succeeded by Gervase Bennett, another Mellor supporter. Mellor, in the meantime, had returned to Derby with his Company, but no sooner had he arrived than he was ordered to joint Poyntz in his operations around Newark. Within hours of his departure, a second writ for the election was delivered to Bennett by Sir George Gresley.

The other side, however, behaved equally unscrupulously. Mellor's brother-in-law, Nicholas Wilmot, approached Thomas Calver, a Gell supporter, and threatened him that "if Captain Mellor be chosen burgess,...be you assured...but that we shall take away all that ever you have, away from you," and Dunnage, meeting Calver by chance some time later told him:

> "He that stands for Mr Gell stands for the Devil, for he is a worthless man and a man of no trust. They that give their voice for him do damn themselves and their posterity to the Pit of Hell."[3]

With such a vicious campaign of character assassination, bullying and intimidation, the election was scarcely likely to be a model of impartiality – it was not. Voting started in the Town Hall on the morning of 9th November. Gell sat by the door and took a note of the burgesses, excluding one for being under age. Outside were gathered some of his soldiers and servants, ready to make an appropriate display of force against Mellor voters. The Mayor (a supporter of Mellor) asked the tellers for the count about half-way through; when it appeared that Mellor was in the lead, he strode to the window, took off his hat and waved it at the crowd outside, shouting "A Mellor, A Mellor". These irregularities were compounded by more glaring ones as the day progressed. A letter arrived from Captain Mellor at Newark signed by 60 of his company wishing to register a vote for him. Gell objected, but the Mayor included them. Desperate measures were called for; at mid-day Thomas Gell's Company of Musketeers deployed in the market place with matches lit, in an attempt to overawe the electorate. Their Lieutenant, Robert Freland, when taxed about their involvement later replied, ingenuously, that "there was no other reason of keeping that company there in arms, but for the security of the garrison the day of the election".

At the end of the day, according to Gell, Mellor had 149 votes and his brother Thomas 170. But this extraordinary affair was not yet over; what appears to have happened is that two returns were supplied to the High Sheriff Gresley, one showing Thomas Gell to have been elected and the other returning Mellor. On their arrival in London, the whole matter was referred to the Committee of Privileges, who after a deliberation of 18 months, and consideration of numerous conflicting and perjured depositions, finally declared Thomas Gell to have been duly returned as Member for the Borough of Derby. This was not until January 1647, but by then Gell's power had been eclipsed, and his influence in County affairs was virtually over.

Inscription at the Crispin Inn, Ashover, commemorating an incident of local fame

Photo: D.J. Mitchell

It can be imagined that the chicanery of the election did little to enhance Gell's tarnished reputation, but it did not lose him, as yet, his military control as governor of Derby and Colonel of the County Parliamentary militia. Although, as we have seen, by May the last main Royalist garrison at Newark had fallen, the early months of 1646 were still busy ones for Gell, for Tutbury Castle, under the command of Gell's old opponent Sir Andrew Kniveton, still held out for the King. On 30th March it was invested by Gell and Brereton, and on 20th April it surrendered on conditions, to the irritation of Cromwell, who considered that Gell had let the garrison off too lightly. By this time too, a flood of petitions had arrived at the Commons complaining of Gell's high-handed behaviour in the conduct of the County's affairs, and Sanders had placed before the Commons Committee for Examinations lengthy articles of impeachment alleging, among other things, peculation of the Committee's funds, plundering and unlawful quartering of soldiers in the Borough and County, failing properly to maintain the garrison at Bolsover and wilfully refusing to attack the enemy when opportunity arose. As a final broadside, the article accused him of being "a frequent swearer, jeerer and scoffer of religious men and practices, a protector of loose and dissolute persons and a persecutor of Godly men".[4] To the "Godly men" of the recruited Long Parliament, these were serious charges, and they stuck; by September 1646 Gell had been deprived of his governorship by the Commons and had left for London to fight his case and petition for repayment of the money he had spent in the cause of the Parliament, according to him some £7,000, on which he was entitled to interest at 8%.

King Charles, in the meantime, had surrendered himself into the custody of the Scots army at Southwell on 5th May 1646 and the first Civil War was virtually over. Parliament's immediate concern, therefore, was to alleviate their very heavy expenditure by disbanding their troops, disgarrisoning their fortifications and destroying any of them likely to afford refuge to Royalists in the event of a Cavalier coup de main or uprising. On 23rd June, Parliament issued orders for the dismantling of defences at Derby and Wingfield Manor. The terse wording of the Ordinance admirably sums up Parliament's priorities now that the fighting in England was finished.

> "The House of Commons have referred the considerations of dismantling Derby, and the imploying of our forces, horse and foot, in the service of Ireland, unto the Commity for the affairs of Ireland, to the intent that ... our countrey may be eased of unnecessary charges and the souldyers employed where there is use of them, hereupon the Committy for the Affairs of Ireland, have thought it fit, that so many of the horse and foot as are willing, shall be entertained into that service, the rest disbanded, and the garrisons (ie defences) of Derby and Wingfield Manor slighted ..."[5]

Eastwood Old Hall, blown up by Sir John Gell's men at the end of the war

Photo: D.J. Mitchell

Surprisingly, at least some of the Derby troops chose to serve in Ireland, where they were commanded by that same Lieutenant Freland as was involved in the Recruiter election, now armed with a Colonel's Commission in the New Model Army.

The defences at Wingfield and Derby were levelled, and the Parliamentarians went on to destroy the Old Hall at Eastwood, garrisoned on its capture in 1643 by Gell's men. It was a sturdy building and they had a little trouble with it, having to resort eventually to blowing it up with gunpowder. This produced a few wry couplets from one Wheatcroft, Clerk to Gell's old friend Emmanuel Bourne of Ashover:-

"The Roundheads came down upon Eastwood Old Hall,
And they tried it with mattock and they tried it with ball,
And they tore up the leadwork and splintered the wood
But as firmly as ever the battlements stood
Till a barrel of powder at last did the thing
And then they sang psalms for the fall of the King."[6]

The relief of the ordinary people of Derbyshire at the end of hostilities after nearly four years must have been tempered by the appearance of that companion of war, plague. By September of 1646 this was everywhere abroad in the Midlands, the Autumn Sessions could not be held, and many people died. But this terrible affliction was soon past, and the year 1647 proved singularly uneventful as the county basked in unaccustomed peace. Elsewhere, however, events were moving inexorably towards tragedy. On 30th January 1647 Charles, after an eight month captivity was handed over to Parliament by the Scots for an indemnity of £200,000 (sufficient to pay the Scots Army's arrears) and went into captivity at Holmby House in Northamptonshire. There followed months of devious and protracted negotations, some secret, some open, between Parliament, the King and the Scots; for much of the period these were accompanied by a spate of rumbling dissatisfactions and mutinies within the New Model Army, whose rank and file and many junior officers were incensed at the proposed disbandment of the army with its arrears of pay undischarged; at this time the regiments of foot were 18 weeks in arrear and the cavalry no less than 43 weeks! The King was able to take advantage of these distractions and on 26th December 1647 he signed the secret 'Engagement' with the Scots whereby he undertook to impose a Presbyterian form of Church Government on England in return for military support.

In February of 1648 the first of a series of Royalist uprisings broke out with the defection of Colonel Poyer in Pembroke, and in the next four months there were outbreaks in Kent, Essex, Yorkshire and South Wales, and a mutiny of the Parliamentary fleet in the Downs. Most of these risings were quickly suppressed, and when the Scots finally stirred themselves and crossed the border on 8th July, the New Model was able to concentrate adequate men to deal with them. They were not aided in their invasion by their General, the Duke of Hamilton, a pompous and vacillating aristocrat of no military talent, and in a running battle between Preston and Warrington, on 17th and 18th August, Cromwell cut them to pieces, killing over 1,000 and taking 7,000 prisoners. Hamilton himself escaped with some of his Scottish horse but was run to earth within days and captured at Uttoxeter with a considerable number of his troops. Some of these unfortunate men were quartered initially in parts of Derbyshire; the county was not fond of Scotsmen, and there were many, particularly in the High Peak, who remembered with bitterness the merciless demands of

Lesley's quartering masters when the Scots army moved into the Midlands after the Battle of Marston Moor; and the weary and bedraggled prisoners met with a hostile, or at best callous, reception. Many of them were shut up in the Church at Chapel-en-le-Frith, and what happened to them there is recorded in a melancholy, but matter-of-fact style, by the Parish Register.

> "1648 – Sept 11. There came to this town of Scots Army, led by the Duke of Hambleton and squandered (sic) by Colonel Lord Cromwell sent hither prisoners from Stopford under the conduct of Marshall Edward Matthews, said to be 1500 in number put into the church Sept 14. They went away Sept 30 following. There were burried of them before the rest went away 44 persons, and more buried Oct 2 who were not able to march, and the same that died by the way before they came to Cheshire 10 and more."[7]

The Second Civil War was a spasmodic affair of separate ill-coordinated and scattered risings, often badly prepared and worse led, and the East Midlands suffered little from its effects. There was, however, one major clash in the area in which at least a troop of Derby horse were involved. A large body of Royalist horse under Sir Philip Monckton and Colonel Gilbert Byron, forced to leave the Royalist garrison at Pontefract for want of provisions, quartered themselves in Doncaster from which they descended into northern Lincolnshire and plundered it. Parliamentarian troops were quickly moved to the area to block the roads south, and by 5th July the Royalists were brought to bay and turned to fight their pursuers in a bean field at Willoughby. There followed a bloody encounter. The Royalists had about 750 men and the Parliamentarians, under Rossiter, perhaps 1,000. The weight of superior numbers told and the Royalists were routed, losing 100 killed, 550 prisoners and all their colours and impedimenta. Rossiter himself was injured as was Captain Greenwood of the Derby troop, the former Governor of the garrison at Barton Park who is described as "dangerously wounded". It is evident, however, that his wounds did not prove fatal; he was promoted to Major the following year, and was still alive in 1662 when he registered arms.

In spite of some hard fighting, the New Model, cured of its mutinous spirit by the prophylactic of battle, managed to suppress the disparate Royalist effort with relative ease, but the effect of the renewed hostilities was predictable and the attitude of Parliament hardened. They viewed the Royalist action as treason, not war, and decided to make an example of the ringleaders. The Duke of Hamilton was tried by his Peers for treason and beheaded. Marmaduke Lord Langdale, the veteran of Naseby and Marston Moor, who had fought with Hamilton at Preston, was captured and incarcerated at Nottingham Castle and only avoided a similar fate by a timely escape to Holland; and at Colchester, which finally surrendered on 28th August, the garrison Commanders, Lucas and Capel, were summarily shot by Fairfax for breach of their parole. The biggest loser, however, was the King. His perfidious arrangement with the Scots was now clearly revealed for all to see, and on 6th January 1649 he went on trial for his life before 135 Commissioners appointed by the House of Commons. The verdict was never in doubt and on 27th January, he was condemned to death for High Treason. On a cold, grey morning three days later, he mounted the scaffold at Whitehall to meet his executioner. An enormous crowd was present to watch this unprecedented event, the legal killing of God's anointed monarch; among the spectators was that same Robert Cotchett whose support of Sanders had led to his banishment from Derby in 1645, and he has left a vivid eyewitness account of the execution in a letter to German Pole of Radbourne which is worth quoting in extenso.

> "The scaffold erected before Whitehall, the King about 2 of the clocke came out of the banqueting house at a passage made through a window upon the scaffold, where the block and axe lay, at which he smilingly looking found fault with the block for being made too lowe. The scaffold was covered with black cloth. His Majestie turned about and spake something to the Bishop of London who replied to him and administered the Lord's supper. I think none heard what was said, but only those few on the scaffold with him, being about 14. Haveing spoke a quarter of an hour he putt off his hat and one of the executioners putt on his head a white capp and gathered upp his hair under it. Then he putt off his doublet and lay flatt downe on his belly with his neck on the block with his arms spread out giving the signe by spreading his hands wider. The executioner, haveing on his knees asked him pardon, cutt off his head at one blow and his mate took it upp and held it up to the spectators which was very many. The executioners were disguised being masqued with great beards and I believe not known to many. The King seemed to dye resolutely. I heard he left a speech in writing to be published. It may be it will come forth the morrow. I shall send it as soon as I can gett it.
>
> All the army was uppon guard at their severall posts at Whitehall, Charing Cross, Westminster, St James parke and fields, Covent Garden etc.
>
> Two Ambassadors at the importunity of the Prince are come from ye States of Holland to intercede but too late. They delivered the message yesterday in French and Dutch to the House, which the House not skilled at required the message in plain English, which is thought but a dilatory complaint on both sides. The Lord Loughborough is escaped from Windsor. There was much scrabbling for the King's blood."[8]

The effect of the King's execution in England and Europe as a whole can scarcely be exaggerated. By this single unprecedented deed the dominant Independent party in Parliament had torn asunder the sinews that had bound the English body politic for 600 years of uninterrupted monarchy. Charles was viewed as a Martyr by the adherents of the Church of England, and many of the Presbyterians, already committed to a compromise with the King that had now been rendered impossible, saw in this deed a final and irrevocable breach between the peace and war factions. From now onwards, Presbyterians would be as active in seeking the overthrow of Cromwell as they had been in seeking the reduction of the King's power. William Sandford, the future Archbishop of Canterbury, eloquently expressed the feelings of most Englishmen in a letter to his brother.

> "The black act is done, which all the world wonders at, and which an age cannot expiate and the waters of the Ocean we swimme in cannot wash out the spotts of yt blood, than which never any was shedd with greater guilt since the sonn of God pour'd out his."

Such an emotional expression of sentiment is alien to us today, but there is little doubt that most Englishmen not of the extreme puritan persuasion, saw the execution of their King, whatever his faults, as an act little short of blasphemy. In the light of this feeling, it is possible to view even the reaction of the eccentric Lord Deincourt as almost normal. Upon hearing of the death of the King, he dug his own grave and each Friday lay down in it dressed in sackcloth in order to meditate and pray, a custom that he pursued with religious devotion until his death some six years later.[9]

10 The Impact of the War

Yor peticioner beinge souldier....receaved such cutts and wounds that ever since he hath lost the use of his arme and hand to his utter undoeing.
A disabled soldier's petition for Poor Relief.

The conclusion of the Second Civil War saw the end of hostilities in Derbyshire to all intents and purposes. The county was not affected by the Third Civil War, although some of its soldiers fought at Worcester, for both Royalists and Parliamentarians, and although the 11 years of the Protectorate saw numerous plots against Cromwell, several of which were hatched in or executed upon the county, its involvement in large-scale fighting was over and it is appropriate, therefore, to consider briefly some aspects of the organization of the two sides in Derbyshire.

In retrospect, the fact that the Parliamentarians triumphed appears almost inevitable. What is surprising is that the Royalists managed to stave off defeat for four long years, amidst every disadvantage that geography and economics could raise against them. It is undoubtedly true, however, that the Parliamentarians' superior organization contributed substantially to their success.

Both sides endeavoured, in the early stages of the war, to base their organization on the existing structure of county government. This centred on the various officials responsible for their counties who were, in the main, appointed by the King. The most important of these was the Lord Lieutenant. Today his function is largely ceremonial, but in the first quarter of the seventeenth century he had very real and extensive powers in the administration of the county. He was, in effect, the King's representative, was appointed by the King alone, and was frequently an eminent local magnate with connections at Court. In Derbyshire, for instance, the Earls of Shrewsbury had, until their decline, provided the local Lords Lieutenant for generations. The rise of the Cavendish family displaced them; in 1628 William Cavendish, 1st Duke of Newcastle, became Lord Lieutenant of the County, a post which he held for ten years until succeeded by his nephew, also William Cavendish, 3rd Earl of Devonshire, who was replaced by John Manners, a parliamentary supporter and 8th Earl of Rutland in 1642, a post in which he continued until the rule of the Major Generals.

The primary function of the Lord Lieutenant was to look to the defence of the county, in which capacity he was responsible for the local militia (the "trained bands") and had control of the county's munitions. He was also responsible for the enforcement of the penal laws against Catholics, the supervision of the collection of forced loans ("Benevolences") and even, as one writer has noted, ascertaining that the King's wishes about the planting of mulberry bushes had been observed. In short he was the King's representative in the county and the county's representative at Court, hence the requirement that he should be a man acceptable to both, with family influence and landed estates in the county.

Working with him, and responsible for such aspects of his function as were delegated to them, were a number of Deputy Lords Lieutenant normally chosen by the Lord Lieutenant himself from among the landed gentry of the county.

Fulfilling the executive functions of the Parliament on a local basis was the High Sheriff, whose job was to put into effect the decisions of the Courts, Quarter Sessions and Assizes, and, more importantly, to carry out the mechanics of some aspects of tax collection. As we have already seen, successive High Sheriffs of Derbyshire were responsible for enforcing the Royal edicts on Ship Money, distraining where necessary on the effects of those reluctant to pay; and it was also their function to assess the tax in such way as they thought fit. The King told them what sum was required; how it was raised and from whom was a matter for the Sheriff. The Sheriffs were appointed annually by the Crown, and were always members of the landed gentry, and often Justices of some seniority.

Lastly, the functions of local government as we understand them today, were fulfilled either by the Corporation, in the case of Charter Boroughs, or by the Magistracy in the case of the county at large. As well as fulfilling their present judicial role, the Magistrates or Justices of the Peace were responsible for enforcing the Poor Laws, supervising public health, maintaining the roads, regulating trade and fixing wages. Indeed, their function in respect of the Poor Law had been increased by an ordinance of the King issued as early as 1631, the so-called "Book of Orders", which constrained the Justices to a close adherence to their duties in that respect, requiring regular reports on the condition of vagabonds, sturdy beggars and idle apprentices within their jurisdictions. This Ordinance was merely one of a number issued by Charles during the period of his personal rule in order to strengthen central control over local affairs.

At the beginning of hostilities, therefore, there was a sophisticated and highly developed system of local administration available to both sides, in order to assist the conduct of the war. In analyzing the methods employed by each side, however, we are hampered by a lack of information about Royalist methods. In Derbyshire, for instance, the Royalists exercised virtually no influence on the county, other than that imposed by their armies whenever they were near enough to control territory, either directly or indirectly. By the nature of things, therefore, such control would tend to be highly centralized and personal, exercised through the person of the Royalist Commander, with little or no control by other bodies save, perhaps, for his Council of War. For example, during the Earl of Newcastle's invasion of the county in the winter of 1643, we find the Earl putting into effect the Commission of Array, billeting soldiers, levying taxes, fixing garrisons, sequestering plate and money, all without so much as a mention of a Committee. What was true of Derbyshire was probably true of other areas under Royalist control. In Newark, for instance, it was the Governor and his Council of War who issued the weekly tax assessments to maintain his troops, and although these were collected through the medium of the Parish Constable, they do not have the appearance of legitimacy that was given by Parliamentary administration with its emphasis on Committees, votes, minutes and other aspects of normal county government.

The Parliamentarians, however, did face substantial problems; for one thing, they were in the same position as the Parliament, being in rebellion against their lawful Sovereign and having, at the same time, to give the impression to both themselves and the outside world, that they were the legitimate authority; hence the constant self-delusion of many Parliamentary ordinances, which talked about opposition to the King's evil counsellors (never the King himself) and were always prefaced as being in support of the King. Take, for example, the preamble to the sequestration ordinance of March 1643:

> "The Lords and Commons assembled in Parliament, taking into their serious consideration the heavy pressures and calamities which now lie upon this kingdom by this unnatural war raised against the Parliament, and that notwithstanding all their faithful and incessant endeavours for the preserving of His Majesty and the whole kingdom from the mischievous and restless designs of Papists and ill affected persons whose aim is the extirpation of our religion, laws and liberties, yet their counsels and practices are still so prevalent with His Majesty, and the hearts of many people so misled and beguiled by their false pretences and insinuations ..."

and so on and so forth. It was therefore of huge importance to the Parliament to give their local administrations both the widest base amongst their supporters, and every possible appearance of legality by using, as far as they could, the existing structures based on the county gentry working in Committee.

In Derbyshire the first Committee was nominated by Parliament in August 1642 in order to raise troops under the Militia Ordinance. It comprised 23 named members and two ex-officio ones, the Mayors of Derby and Chesterfield for the time being. Predictably it included three of the county's four MPs (Coke, Curzon and Hallowes but not Allestree who was Royalist), Gell, his brother Thomas, his friend Gresley, and his son-in-law Henry Wigfall. The Treasurer was Nathaniel Hallowes. This first Derbyshire Committee was also empowered by the Ordinance of

Willm Bradford
Robert [illegible] Paid of by order
Geo Eyre Paid of, for Ireland
Edward Worrall Red: ye order, but had Horse & Armes
Adam Woodcock
Ed. [illegible]
Antho [illegible] Red [illegible] ye order but had noe Horse
Jo Hindley Paid of ye order
Tho Gregory Red ye order, but had Ho: & Armes
Jo Blackwell Paid of by order, for Ireland
Jo Bagley Paid of by ord, for Ireland
Hugh [illegible] Ran away to Gen Poinitz
Ed. Stanley Paid of by order
Jo Newton Red ye order, but had Ho: & armes
Robert Harison
Jo Montross Ran away with Ho: & Armes to Scotts
Robert Cate Ran away to Scotts with Ho Armes
[illegible] Ran away to ye Scotts and
Patrick Maguire [illegible] listed under Hamilton
Jo Bradley, Paid of by order.
Jo Bullocke
[illegible] Watt Paid of by order
Rich [illegible] Paid of by order
Tho Palmer Paid of by order
Rich Ellaston
[illegible]

Part of a roll of the men in Sir John Gell's Company as listed in 1645, with notes on what became of them by October 1646. Some had joined the Scots army; some had volunteered for service in Ireland; others had simply been "paid of by order"

Derbyshire Record Office D258/31/30y. From the archives of the Chandos-Pole-Gell Family, deposited in Derbyshire Record Office

Jo: williamson — The mony Paid his wife, but he was slaine
Tho Beckett
Geo: Smith
Geo: Taylor
willm Rose — Laide downe his Armes:
Ed Holme — Laid downe Armes
willm Asley
Gilbert Atkins (was slaine at [illegible] his
Rich Howfeild (wiff 6 more she hath one of them,
Tho Beele
Robert Atkins Red: as ye order
Robert Bonnington, Ran awaye, to the Scotts.
James Adams
willm Jefferys [illegible] Ran awaye to Leister Regiment
Antho Gale Paid of by order
Rich Heshop
Giles Carter
Jo Lomas — Red as ye order, But had Ho: & Arm
Tho Allen, went to Capt walshes Troope: Ho: A
Math, Elwood, went wth Ho: & Armes to Gen Poyntz
Ed Sydney — went to Hambleton Troope
Jo Upton — Paid of for Ireland
Gilbert Bonder, Laid downe Armes
Rich Taylor; went into [illegible] —

November 1642, to raise money, arms and plate by means of voluntary contributions and loans upon which interest would be payable at 8%. In the town of Derby this produced a total of £1,254-2-0 from 79 contributors, from £1-0-0 given by Henry Fletcher up to £60 given by Edward Wilmot. Gervase Bennett contributed an ungenerous £6-17-4 and the Mayor, Henry Mellor, £30.[1] It soon became clear, however, that mere voluntary contributions would be insufficient and on 24th February 1643 Parliament passed an Ordinance levying a weekly tax or assessment on each county according to its presumed means. This is an interesting guide to the relative wealth of different areas; the poorer areas paid the least, Merionethshire being assessed at a mere £12-10-0 per week, while Kent was to pay £1,250 and Devon, then generally accepted as the wealthiest county, a massive £1,800 weekly. Derbyshire's contribution was £175 per week, and it was in the apportionment and collection of this tax, which remained until the Restoration, that the main purpose of the Committee lay. In theory the Parliament was to take two-thirds of the amount collected, the remaining third being used by the county for its own purposes. In practice, however, many counties kept a good deal more than that, and disbursed their expenses locally.

The Committee, or any two members of it, was empowered to appoint assessors and collectors as they saw fit, and there is little doubt that in Derbyshire, as elsewhere, the members of the County Committee saw in these wide powers an opportunity to both enrich themselves and to pay off old scores. Gell himself was heavy-handed with those he considered to be his personal enemies, and the collection of arms, money and plate was carried out with ruthless indifference on friends and enemies alike. The most quoted example of Gell's methods is his raid on the Stanhopes at Elvaston, which was reported in the Royalist Newspaper Mercurius Aulicus on 15th February 1643. It gives every indication that the raising of money from the Stanhopes was in no way "voluntary" and can scarcely be distinguished from outright plunder.

> "Sir John Gell with his forces consisting of about 400 men came to Elvaston in Derbyshire, home of the Lady Stanhope, widow of Sir John Stanhope, to whom Gell (though never a friend), yet in his lifetime durst not declare himself an enemy. But after his death, making use of the power given him by the fundamental laws of the kingdom, he plundered his house of all the arms, money and goods of worth he could find, to the value of £1,500. Not contented with this, and to make it more plainly appear that his coming was as much for malice as plunder, he went into the garden (in which the good lady, taking very much delight, had made it a very pleasant place, with handsome walks and diversities of the best flowers), which he caused to be digged up and utterly ruined. He left not here, but to add more to her vexation, and to please himself in doing mischief, he went into the church, where she had lately erected a tomb for her husband which cost

her £500, that he caused to be demolished, and the stones to be broken into several pieces, that no possibility was left to repair it. But his act of greatest inhumanity was to go with his soldiers into the vault, where the dead of the family were usually buried, and to run their swords through their dead bodies."[2]

There is little here of the loyalty and moderation upon which Parliament laid such emphasis, and although the incident quoted is unusual in its brutal vindictiveness, it is only one example of many irregularities perpetrated by the County Committee, or Gell personally, during his four years as Governor of Derby. It is clear, for example, that looting of Royalist sympathizers on a large scale was commonplace in the early days of the war, and there is little doubt that the proceeds benefitted Gell as much as the Parliamentary cause. A little earlier in the year, for instance, the Mayor of Derby received a letter of complaint from the inhabitants of Melbourne, Repton and other villages in the south-west of the county:

> "...we cannot but take notice of the forces lately raised by Sir John Gell who have their residence within the towne of Derbie; and from thence issue into divers parts of this county, to the great suffering of many, and to the terror and affrightment of others; as in particular the great prejudice donne to the Earl of Chesterfield at Bretby, to the value of many thousand pounds; and since taken from Mr Sacheverall of Morely, £3000 in money, besides horses and other goodes; and from Mr Gylbert of Lockoe, to the value of £200; and from many of us, and our neighbours' horses comeing to the markett, which caused divers to throw off their sacks of corne upon the way, and return home; so that we dare not come to your markett to sell our commodities, nor can we assure ourselves of safetie at home."[3]

During its first ten months, the Committee's Accounts were kept by its Treasurer, Nathaniel Hallowes, who received £10,563–4–3 and spent £124–4–3 more than this. Given that in the first two months of 1643, Gell had plundered no less than £4,700 from Gilbert, the Earl of Chesterfield and the Stanhopes alone, not counting other seizures and the weekly assessment of £175, it is clear that there are major discrepancies between monies received by Gell and monies that passed through the Account Books of the Committee; and it is equally clear that these defalcations increased as the war went on. Of course, the Royalists did the same when they got the chance, as witness the plundering of Gell's home at Hopton by the Knivetons, and it is possible to understand, even if not to condone, Gell's attempts to recover and safeguard his position by using the same tactics.

After the surrender of the Royalist garrisons at Wingfield and Bolsover, more regular and efficient collection of the weekly assessment was possible; each Hundred had a Receiver appointed to it, to whom the Constables of the Parishes had to account, and the Committee exercised a supervisory role, sometimes travelling in a body to one part of the county or another. These peripatetic exercises in tax collection were not, however, without their dangers; parts of the county were still subject to cavalry raids from the Royalist garrison at Newark, and on one memorable occasion the entire County Committee was captured at Wirksworth, an incident wryly noted by Sir Samuel Luke in a letter to the Earl of Essex.

> "28th February 1645 ... on Tuesday morning last, the Committee for Derbyshire met at Wirksworth, 24 miles from Newark, being guarded by 120 horse, and raising monies, were surprised by a party from Newark, and the Committee and the 120 horse taken together with about £1,000 which they had collected, and were all carried safe to Newark."[4]

They must have been subsequently exchanged, but unhappily there is no record of this. It is safe to assume, however, that the incident caused no little embarrassment to Gell, and doubtless considerable amusement and profit to the Newark Royalists!

At local level, there is an interesting insight into the work of the County Committee in the papers of the Constable of Hope, a little village in the High Peak. These comprise some twenty-five letters from the County Committee to the Constable from October 1644 onwards. The following, written in late October 1644, is a typical example:-

> To the Constable of Hope,
> Theise are to charge and command you to give warning to all psons within your Constablery as well freeholders as others that are possessed of lands, stocks of money or other goods, that they appeare befower two or more of us at Chappell in le Fryth at Nick Smythe's house upon Satterday next to compound with us for ye fifth pte of theire yearly revenew and twentieth pte of theire personall estate according to the ordinances of Parliament. And likewise that you give warning to all the severall tennants within your said Constablery belonging to the Earles of Newcastle, Devonshire, Row Eyre of Hassop, John Milward, John Shalcrosse Esquires that they bring in theire rents at the tyme and place abovesaid and pay the same to us or to whom we shall appoint to be imployed for ye present service of the Parliament
>
> | | |
> |---|---|
> | Tho Saunders | John Gell |
> | Robt Eyre | Geo Gresley |
> | J Wigfall | Theo Gell[5] |
> | Jo Wigley | |

It is important to note that the landowners mentioned by name in the letter were all prominent Royalists whose estates would have been sequestered by Parliament thus making their tenants liable to pay rent to the County Committee rather than the individual landlord. It is clear, however, that there was a wide gulf between theory and practice. Paying taxes is never popular and in the conditions of the Civil War when exorbitant demands were made by both sides and plundering and free-quartering became the norm, it is not to be wondered at that there was a certain amount of resistance, as the following letter shows:

> "Mr Stayley,
> The contempt of your p'decessor is not yet remitted and if you faile in the execucon of this warrant as formerly I shalbe enforced to use extreamities which I abhorre. I shall sitt noe more but ye day p'fixed in the warrant, one whereof which is to Hathersadge I desire to be sent forthwith the other way, every effort to be executed whereby there may not be any longer abused the patience of yor truly lo(ving) friend if your manner give not otherwise.
> John Bretland
> 10 January 1644(1645)
> I have staded till Friday in the afternoone at Chappell expecting the execucon of yor last warrant. Let this ltre be delivered to Mr Balgue. I fear I shall be enforced to make you a precedent: for yor father's sake I desire not."[6]

On the whole, however, the system of administration and particularly of taxation imposed on the county by the parliamentary side during the Civil War appears to have worked adequately in spite of its not infrequent failings and abuses. At all events it worked sufficiently well to ensure continued parliamentary domination of the county throughout the period, notwithstanding the presence of a large body of Royalist sympathizers within the county boundaries, many of whom were actively in arms.

The Royalists, on the other hand, seem to have been unable to establish any substantial measure of administrative control over the areas of the county dominated by them. This was due in part to the fact that they had been excluded early on from the county government by parliamentary supporters like Gell and Curzon; their only MP, Allestree, left the county to join the King at Oxford at the start of hostilities and the remaining royalist gentry had little or no access to the levers of power. Whilst they were able to control small areas from time to time by military force, this was never enough decisively to tip the balance of power in the county. It must be said, however, that this was not a problem unique to Derbyshire; it was faced by Royalists everywhere except in those parts of the country where their support was total – the ability of the parliamentary side effectively to use and centrally direct the organs of local government was in large measure responsible for their ultimate success.

What, then, of the impact of the war in Derbyshire in terms of life and property? In the absence of accurate and detailed statistics, it is a task beset by difficulties to do anything more than give a rough and ready guide to the cost of the conflict in the locality. A recent historian has estimated that the total cost of the war in lives was about 100,000 out of a population of approximately 3,000,0000 or one-in-thirty.[7] Applying this to Derbyshire's population of 60,000, therefore, would give us a figure of 2,000 dead as a direct and indirect result of the hostilities. This is not too far out from an exercise that I carried out some years ago and which gave a total of about 1,500 dead over the period from 1642 to 1651. To put the figure into context, if we apply those figures, say, to the present day population of Derby City, we have a total mortality of about 7,300.

It will readily be seen, therefore, that in human terms the cost was enormous. The county, although it saw no large scale battles, was heavily involved in the fighting from the very start. Gell's assistance to the surrounding counties, particularly Staffordshire and Nottinghamshire, resulted in heavy and constant casualties to his troops. The Battle of Hopton Heath alone meant one hundred or more dead to the Derbyshire Parliamentarians and on the Royalist side, the Derbyshire Regiments of Freschville, Eyre, Milward and Shallcross must have sustained several hundred casualties, a high proportion of them killed, at the Battle of Marston Moor. Sieges such as Newark and Wingfield inevitably meant large casualties particularly as the Derbyshire troops usually found themselves in the position of having to attack in the open while the defenders were ensconced behind their defences.

Mary Spencer her husband being a souldier was
slayne in ye parliament service, and hath
a childe to mayntayne
therefore prayeth releife.

A request to the County J.P.s for relief for Mary Spencer, a soldier's widow who "hath a child to mayntayne"

Derbyshire Record Office QSB641. From the records of Derbyshire Quarter Sessions, reproduced by permission of Derbyshire Record Office

Added to these major actions was the constant daily round of skirmish and ambush, particularly in and around the Royalist garrisons adjoining the county and Parliamentarian garrisons established to block them. Barton Hall, for instance, was garrisoned in October 1644 to oppose the Royalist stronghold at Tutbury and the surrounding area was ravaged by fighting, for months thereafter, between Gell's 700 horse and the active Royalists of Tutbury under Sir Andrew Kniveton (he who had plundered Gell's estates at the beginning of the war). The Cavalier diarist Richard Symonds was involved in a fight with the Barton garrison in August 1645 during the King's retreat from Naseby.

> "In this march (from Tutbury to Ashbourne) a body of 500 of the enemies horse fell upon our reare, neare Barton garrison, by Tedbury; were well received by us, twenty of ours hurt, three or four on both sides kill'd; we toke twelve prisoners and lost some, and a captain."[8]

As well as the toll of dead and wounded in battle, there were the usual accompaniments of war – accident, lawlessness and disease. In the records of All Saint's Church, Derby for April 1644 there is the following entry "Catherine Gower killed with a pistoll bullet, shot through the head by a acedent"[9] and in the Register of Longford Church there is mention of a murder committed by local soldiers.

> "John Malley was attacked and had his house broken in sundry places by souldiers the first of November in the night, and because they could not get in and he would not yield, they shot him with a sluge into the head, and soe died and was buried the 2nd day of November."[10]

The plight of the wounded in seventeenth century battles was particularly severe; medical treatment was rudimentary and there was no understanding of the importance of anti-sepsis. Bullet wounds in joints or which affected the internal organs were usually fatal. There were however, limited medical facilities available, often provided by barber surgeons or the clergy. There is an interesting manuscript in the Public Record Office which casts some light on the care of the wounded, a bill for medical attention to some members of the Barton garrison after a skirmish in July 1645. The George Blagrave mentioned was the Clerk of All Saints Church, Derby.

> "A true note of all those wounded soldiers cured by George Blagrave and his sonne since his last bill for which he demandeth pay as follows:-

	£	s	d
Imprimis – At the fight near Ashe on Tuesday the first of July John Cox 1 cut in his hand and a very soare wound in his arm ...	1	0	0
Hugh Bande of Capt. Barton's, a thrust in the arm with a tuck and a shott in the back ...	1	3	4
John Bullock of Capt. Barton's, a very sore cut in the forepart of his head which caused a piece of his skull the breadth of a half a crowne peace to [be] taken forth, also a very sore cut over his hand ...	1	10	0
William Higgott of Major Molynes [Molanus] companye a sore bruised legge ...	1	0	0
Richard Hudson taken prisoner at Ashby haveing a sore cut in the shoulder was sent to be dressed by the governor's command ...		6	8
One John Curson a Scotsman, Quartermaster a very sore wound in the head ...	1	0	0
Robert Morris of Major Sander's his comp haveing a dangerous cut over the eye hurt at Keyworth and a sore thrust through the arme ...	1	0	0
Luke Severne quartermaster Capt Hope a thrust and cut in the arme a very dangerous wound ...	1	0	0
Richard Becke of Liefftenant Cornalls, a very sore scalded foot ...		5	0
For cureing 10 cavaliers taken at the fight at Ashe whereof one was shot in the arme in the elbowe joynt and the bullet taken forth in the wrist near the hand. The rest were sore cut in their heads and thrust in the back. Cavaliers of Newark ...	5	0	0"[11]

The dead and wounded were not, of course, the only victims. Material losses were also very great. In April of 1643 Parliament took steps to forfeit the estates of Royalists in arms and their sympathizers. The system of forfeiture was organized centrally in London by the Committee for Compounding and its functions were delegated to local committees in each county who were expected to seize and forfeit the estates of active Cavaliers (delinquents as they were known) and arrange for the disposal of their lands and chattels. Two-thirds of the money thus raised was to be remitted to London, the remaining one third being retained by the County Committee for its own expenditure. In certain circumstances it was possible for a repentant Royalist to buy back his estates at an agreed proportion of its value (the greater his offence the higher the price) and this was known as 'compounding'.

In Derbyshire the machinations of the local committee affected virtually every Royalist family in the county.[12] The first members of the

Sequestration Committee included the most active members of the County Committee, namely Sir John Curzon, Sir John Gell, Sir John Coke, Francis Revel, Nathaniel Hallowes (the County Treasurer) and James Abney, and they set to work immediately. The largest local landowners and wealthiest Royalists by far were the Cavendish family, William 3rd Earl of Devonshire and William 1st Duke of Newcastle. The losses of the Duke of Newcastle through sequestration and personal expenditure on his troops during the war reached a total of £950,000, an enormous sum at the time, perhaps equivalent now to something in excess of £200,000,000.[13] His estates in the county were seized and sold at 5½ years purchase by the local commissioners raising £111,593 for Parliament. His cousin William, Earl of Devonshire, fled to France in 1642 and was not so much involved in the war. He returned and submitted in 1645 and was fined £5,000 and pardoned.

These depredations, however, were not confined only to the aristocracy or the very wealthy; they permeated every level of society. Among those affected in the county were Sir John Harpur of Swarkestone who compounded for his estates in the (huge) sum of £4,000, John Milward of Snitterton, £1,000, the eccentric Lord Deincourt £1994–12–7, right down to George Eyre of Hathersage £25 and John Miles of Ednaston, a humble ten shillings.[14]

Some prominent county families who supported the King, the Cockaynes for example, never really recovered from the fines and taxes levied on them during the war, and even the very wealthy must occasionally have found it difficult to recover from such enormous penalties. The Duchess of Newcastle reckoned that her husband lost £45,000 in felled timber and some tens of thousands of pounds of personal chattels quite apart from the loss of rents over some seventeen years from his exile after the Battle of Marston Moor until the Restoration of 1660.[15]

In summary, it can be fairly said that the period of the Civil Wars was probably the single greatest trauma suffered by the county in his history, not excluding the First World War. The fatal casualties were greater per capita, and many were left maimed and disabled; the great houses of the county had nearly all seen fighting and many had been garrisons for the King or Parliament. Old Chatsworth was variously a Royalist garrison and a Parliamentarian one and suffered accordingly as did Wingfield and Bolsover. The houses of the lesser county gentry also sustained considerable damage. Shalcross Hall, Wingerworth, Tissington, Bretby, Swarkestone and Barton House were all garrisons at one time or another and were assaulted by artillery fire, stormed or plundered. The ordinary folk of Derbyshire had had to suffer four years of bitter fighting and the county was fortunate not to be significantly involved in the Second or Third Civil Wars of 1648 and 1650 to 1651. However, the petitions by wounded soldiers and others that continued to be presented to the Quarter Sessions for, in some cases, the

To the Right Hon: and Wor his Maties Justices of the Peace for the County of Darby at their Quarter Sessions Assembled

The humble Petition of John Brocklehurst of Alderwasley in the said County Labourer humbly sheweth

Whereas yor said Petitioner haveinge beene a Souldier for his late Matie of ever Blessed Memory: under the Command of Captaine John Lowe of Alderwasley in the said County Esq lately deceased, and in the said service receiving hurts and Bruises: togather with old Age beinge become altogather uncapeable of obtaineinge a Livelyhood by his hard labor, and beinge informed his Maties is Graciously pleased to bestow Pensions of Faithfull & Loyall Indigent Souldiers: yor Petitioner humble request is That yor Honours and Worships would be pleased to allowe him such a proportion as you in yor Judicious Judgment shall thinke meete and convenient for an object of soe much pitty ..

And yor Petitioner as bound shall ever pray .

Petition of John Brocklehurst of Alderwasley, an old Royalist soldier, "uncapeable of obtaineinge a livelyhood by his hard labour"

Derbyshire Record Office QSB645. From the records of Derbyshire Quarter Sessions, reproduced by permission of Derbyshire Record Office

next forty years, bear eloquent testimony to the suffering caused to individuals and families by the most prolonged and serious civil war ever suffered by our country. Let one example from the Quarter Session records of 1649 suffice:

> "The Humble Petition of James Cawverd, Maymed soldier Sheweth that about 5 years agoe yor peticioner beinge souldier under the command of Coll. Randle Ashenhurst in the p'liament's service beigne one of a p'tie by order apointed to keepe the hall at Shallcrose: Mr Shallcrosse himself entringe the house and a strong p'tie with him cutt and wounded most of the souldiers found in the house: Amongst whom yor peticioner receaved such cutts and wounds: that ever since he hath lost the use of his arme and hand to his utter undoeinge ... in comisieracon whereof ... may it please yor wor'pps ... to appoint that yor peticioner may receave such yerely stipend ... as you shall think fitt towards the reliefe of himself his wife and children."[16]

How then can we view this turbulent period in the county's history? It is perhaps best expressed in the words of one of the participants. Emmanuel

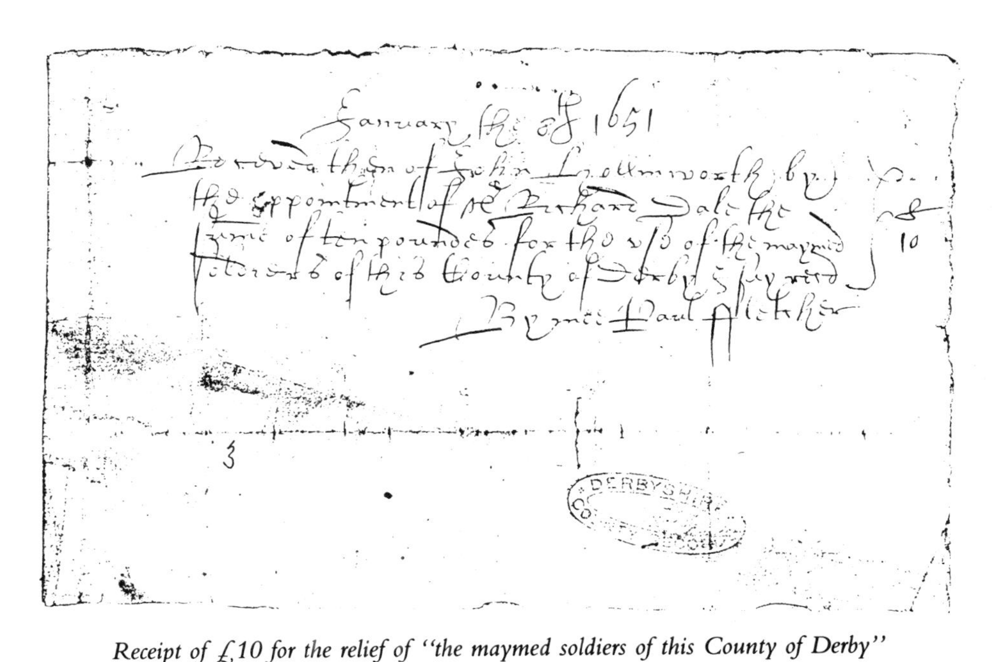

January the 8th 1651
Received then of John Hollinworth by the appointment of Mr Richard Dale the summe of ten poundes for the use of the maymed souldiers of this County of Derby I say recd
By mee Paul Fletcher

10

Receipt of £10 for the relief of "the maymed soldiers of this County of Derby"

Derbyshire Record Office QSB666. From the records of Derbyshire Quarter Sessions, reproduced by permission of Derbyshire Record Office

Bourne the Presbyterian Rector of Ashover. Writing to one of his relatives in August 1646, in a letter full of character and insight he says:

> "In the beginning of the yeare of grace 1642, when I saw both sydes bent on war and destruction, I made up my mynde to take part with neither, but to attend to my two parishes and leave them to fighte it out ... I think both sides were to blame; the Parliament went too far, and the King could not be justified; for indeed he had done harm in favouring the Papists and in exacting taxes not sanctioned by Parliament."

He then appends a neat summary of the war and concludes with a vivid description of the destruction of his home by the Parliamentarian troops.

> "The next daye a companie of dragoones, under the charge of a Muster Master named Smedley, came to the hall and demanded possession in the name of the High Court of Parliament, which I at once did give, but I told them that I had done nothing against the Parliament, and that I was also holding office under their highnesses at the tyme, and that I should bring their conduct before either Fairfax or Col. Hutchinson; but they replied with all civility that they had orders from their commanding officer to destroy the hall, and that he had also said he would not leave a nest in the countrie where a malignant could hyde his head. They, however, offered to assist me in removing anything I set store bye.
>
> I now found that they had brought three small pieces of ordnance, which they drew to the top of Ferbrick, and discharged them at the hall; but the cannons being small (only two drakes and one saker) they did no harm beyond breaking the windows and knocking off the corners of the walls, and they soon tyred and sett the pioneers; but the walls being thick and the mortar good, they made little progress, till at last, growing impatient, they did put a barrel of powder in the tower, and at once destroyed more than halfe the hall and left the other in ruins, so that it cannot be repaired. They then sung a psalm, marched to the church, and for fear they should injure the house of God, I did soon follow after, and to my great surprise did find the scout-master Smedley in the pulpit, when he did preach a sermon two hours long about Popery, Priestcraft, and Kingcraft; but Lord! what stuff and nonsense he did talke, and if he could have murdered the Kyng as easily as he did the Kyng's English, the war would long since have been over: then singing a psalm they prepared to go, but some of the pyoneers seeing the stayned windows once belonging to the Reresbys, on which was paynted the crucifixion, they said it was rank popery and must be destroyed: so they brought their mattocks and bars, and not only destroyed the glass but the stonework also. They then found out the prayer-booke, and surplice and the old parish-registere, which had been hid in the vestrie, but the registere being old and partly in Latin, they could not read it, so they said it was full of popery and treason, and tooke the whole to the market-place, and making a fyre, did burn them to ashes.
>
> (And then)

> The destruction of my house, however, has almost broken my heart, and I trust you will joyn me in praying for better times, and for grace and patience to bear my misfortunes with resignation."[17]

His words could stand as an epitaph for all those who lost family property and youth in those distracted times.

11 The World Turned Upside Down

They said: Take him away gaoler and cast him into the dungeon amongst the rogues and felons; which they then did and put me in the dungeon amongst thirty felons in a lousy, stinking low place in the ground, without any bed.
George Fox on his treatment in Derby.

The execution of the King and the triumph of the Independent faction within Parliament, hurled the country headlong into a whirling void of uncertainty in which radical opinions of every hue, some of them exceedingly bizarre, flourished and spread like wildfire. Some were overtly political in emphasis, such as the Levellers, who will be dealt with in the next chapter; some were amalgams of both religious and political views, such as those expressed by the Fifth Monarchy Men who believed in an imminent second coming of the Messiah and, in preparation for it, wished to establish a theocratic political structure such as that envisaged and partly realized by Calvin in Geneva; but in the main the theories, attitudes and ideas given free vent and expression by the English Revolution were fundamentally religious. In other words, given the perceptions of the seventeenth century man, he was infinitely more concerned about his own individual salvation than about the sort of society in which he lived.

Of course, the theological and the political frequently overlapped and, indeed, clashed. As in Luther's Germany and the England of Queen Elizabeth, it was found to be impossible to divide a man's conscience from his political allegiance. A Catholic to Elizabeth was generally synonymous with an attachment to Spanish interests and, given the unequivocal terms of the Pope's Bull, Regnans in Excelsis,[1] no Catholic could be expected to give undivided loyalty to a Queen who had been declared not only a bastard and a usurper, but, more to the point, a heretic. In the German states, over which Charles V exercised an uneasy and frequently contested power, the rise of Lutheran doctrines were, to Charles and his successors, merely a convenient peg upon which their over-mighty subjects could hang their hats under the pretence of freedom of conscience. And so it was in Cromwell's Republic. Born out of rebellion and the murder of the King, the triumphant Republicans of 1650 were overshadowed by an awareness of their own essentially illegitimate origins; the execution of Charles Stuart had opened the Pandora's Box of radicalism, and the Parliament tried desperately to shut the lid. Far from being liberal in its religious views, the

Parliament was, if anything, more oppressive even than the Arminian clerics that brought down the wrath of the Long Parliament on their heads, and resulted in the execution of Archbishop Laud.

The English Revolution is frequently looked upon as a brief, but heady, triumph of the common people. It was nothing of the sort; like the French Revolution, it was, in essence, a victory for the bourgeoisie. The Rump Parliament contained very few butchers, bakers and candlestick makers, but a great many lawyers, including Cromwell, and even more members of the minor landed gentry. As such their prime concern was to impose order on a country in turmoil after nearly eight years of war, and of course religious uniformity was viewed as synonymous with political unity. Parliament attempted to impose this uniformity in part through the abolition of the episcopacy. This was inevitable. Indeed the Solemn League and Covenant of September 1643, which had brought in the Scots on the side of Parliament, bound the signatories to

> "endeavour the extirpation of Popery, prelacy (that is, Church government by archbishops, bishops, their chancellors and commissaries, deans, deans and chapters, archdeacons, and all other ecclesiastical officers depending on that hierarchy) superstition, heresy, schism, profaneness and whatsoever shall be found to be contrary to sound doctrine and the power of godliness ... that the Lord may be one and his name one in the three kingdoms."

The question was, what to put in its place.

As early as June 1643, Parliament had established a convocation of divines to consider the religious question. Known as the Westminster Assembly, it was composed of 121 Ministers, 10 members of the House of Lords and 20 Members of the Commons, with a large majority in favour of the Presbyterian form of Church organization. For the next six years, it constantly debated the issues amidst the ever-increasing confusion of war, peace, renewed war and the execution of the King, but made little headway. The problem was that there was no consensus in the country at large as to the direction that the Church of England should take; many members, of course, even those who were Parliamentary supporters, still favoured episcopacy. Although by 1646 the Presbyterian faction were in a powerful political position, this was weakened over the next three years by the increasing unpopularity of the Scots. Their depredations in the northern parts of the country which they occupied, their increasingly dictatorial attitude over both political and religious issues, and ultimately their double-dealing with the King and their invasion of England in his support at the beginning of the Second Civil War, all combined to reduce Presbyterianism as a political force. Coupled with this was the rise in Independency, supported by Oliver Cromwell, who was a passionate advocate of religious toleration, provided, of course, that it was not extended to Catholics or the Fifth Monarchy Men! The Independent Sects, which were particularly well-represented within the New Model Army, viewed askance any form of National Church Government, and even, in some cases, the prospect that Ministers would have to be ordained; they sought to reduce to the barest minimum any human agency that might interfere between a man's conscience and his God.

The effect of all this dissension was that the introduction of Presbyterianism was patchy, incomplete and infinitely variable between one part of the country and another. By 1646, although Parliament, on the recommendation of the Westminster Assembly, had introduced a Directory of Worship to replace the Book of Common Prayer, that hallowed rite remained unabolished; although they had postulated a form of Presbyterian Church organization, Bishops and Archbishops were left unaffected by statute, and although several ordinances both defined the organization and provided for it to be put into effect, little attempt was made to do this outside of London.

But in Derbyshire there seems to have been the will and the means to establish much more fully a complete form of Presbytarian Church organization, as laid down by the Westminster Assembly. This provided for a hierarchical structure starting at the bottom with the Parish Presbytery which comprised a Minister "to preach and rule", a body of Lay Elders "to rule but not preach" and Deacons to administer to the needs of the poor. This was aptly described as "a republic complete in itself". The next stage up was a "Classical Assembly", commonly known as a Classis which was more or less equivalent to a diocese and covered a considerable number of parishes from the same area. It was composed of not more than 4 and not less than 2 delegates from each parish, plus the Minister and it was directed by a Moderator, an elective office whose membership was chosen by those present at each meeting. The function of the Classis was, among other things, to "admit candidates to office" (in other words, to ordain Ministers) and to supervise and control the ministers and elders within its jurisdiction. It could also lay down the procedure for examining candidates for ordination, although this had to be within the spirit of Parliaments's Ordinance of August 1646 which required candidates to be twenty-four years of age, to take the Solemn League and Covenant, to be diligent in their lives and modest in their conversations, and to possess a University Degree in Theology. They were expected to undergo a searching examination into their competence in Greek, Hebrew and Latin, and to demonstrate their skill in theological disputation and the preaching of sermons. Above the Classis there was intended to be Provincial Assembly, and, at the top of the tree, a National Assembly but in fact neither of these bodies was ever convened.

In Derbyshire Classes were established for each hundred; these met at Wirksworth for the Low Peak, Chesterfield for Scarsdale, Bakewell and

Glossop for the High Peak, Derby for Morleston and Litchurch, Repton or Melbourne for Gresley and Breadsall for Appletree.

Fortunately for us the Minute Book of the Wirksworth Classis has been preserved,[2] and this gives a unique insight into the workings of one of the few fully established Classes in the entire country, for the period of the early 1650's. I am bound to say, however, that whilst it has very considerable historical importance, it is about as exciting as reading one's way through a complete run of the average Parish Magazine! That in itself, though, speaks volumes as to the stulifying and oppressive hand that Presbyterianism laid upon the county, and the speed and vigour with which its dull routines and killjoy precepts were flung off at the earliest opportunity. Because, be it remembered, Parliament by this time had forbidden most of the pleasures dear to the Englishman's heart; gaming with cards was abolished, as was bear and bull-baiting, stage plays, the maypole, dancing and even Christmas and travelling on a Sunday. There were, furthermore, regular fasts which in Derbyshire were held on the second Thursday of each month.

The Classis was nearly always held at Wirksworth but once each at Ashbourne, Crich and Kniveton, and the most active Moderators were Mr Coates (Minister of South Wingfield) who was appointed on 21 occasions, Mr Watkinson of Kirk Ireton, (19 occasions) Mr Shelderdale of Crich and Matlock, (16 occasions) and Mr Oldfield of Carsington, (15 occasions). Here is a somewhat more lively entry than usual, showing the Classis engaged on their favourite pursuit of wagging their fingers at evil-doers.

> "18th May 1652 – This day Mr John Wiersdall, Minister of Bradley, upon summons … appeared before the Classis, where it was layd to his charge that he had admitted not onlie only [sic] his own people p'imiscouslie to the Sacrament of the Lord's Supper but also some others of the Parish of Wirksworth who were not thought fitt to be received in their own Congregacon. And also that he had spoken disgracefully of some private meetings of Godly and peaceable men and women who joyning with the Publicke Congregacons in all Ordinarries did yet desire to meet together in the weeke day for their mutual edifications spending the time in fasting and pray'r."[3]

Having "ingennouslie confessed and acknowledged" his fault, the Classis ordered that

> "Mr Peter Watkinson should, … in all Brotherlie manner give him some gentle reproof for his form'r miscariage … earnestlie exhort him according to his p'mise to act more carefully and regularly in the admin. of the Lord's Supper and to have a more tender respect to Godly people in reference to their private meetings being no wayes in contempt of a prejudice to the publicke."[4]

Much more exciting than the plodding bureaucracy of the Presbytery were the various sects that the new air of radicalism spawned and encouraged. Many of these involved an element of mystical enlightenment on the part of the convert, and trance-like revelation and heightenend spiritual awareness was encouraged.

The Sects were many and varied; Ranters, Diggers, Shakers, all enjoyed a brief period of liberty and opportunity to propogate their ideas, but one was destined to be more than merely a passing phase, the Quakers, and they flourished and took root in the remote hill farms and valleys of Derbyshire.

Their founder was George Fox, a weaver's son born at Drayton in the Clay in Leicestershire in 1624. In his "Journal" Fox describes himself as having "a gravity and stayedness of mind and spirit not usual in children" and indeed he would need every ounce of his considerble moral courage in the years that followed. In his teens he was apprenticed to a local shoemaker and wool dealer but, constantly troubled in his mind and spirit, he eventually abandoned his friends and family in September 1643 and took to wandering up and down the country, meeting and disputing with Ministers and laypeople and gradually defining his own views of Christianity and salvation and the relation between man and God. In 1647 he first entered Derbyshire "moved by the Lord" as he puts it, and apparently made some converts there – "I met with some friendly people" he says, "and had many discourses with them. Then passing further into the Peak country, I met with more friendly people, and with some in empty high notions". This last remark is typical of Fox, and is the sort of brutally frank observation that was to land him in difficulty so frequently. By 1650 he had already established small cells of converts, mainly in the North and Midlands, and in October he was back in Derby again staying with a local physician and his family who were converts to the faith. On 30th October, he attended a service at All Saints. One of the preachers was Colonel Nathaniel Barton. When the sermons were over Fox says "I spake to them what the Lord commanded me of the Truth and the day of the Lord and the light within them and the spirit to teach and lead them to God: and they were pretty quiet". As well they might be! The church authorities at All Saints had never before encountered quite such a situation and were evidently in a quandary as to how to deal with it. The outcome was predictable however, and Fox with his two companions, one of whom was John Fretwell of Stainsby, were arrested for blasphemy and sent to the Derby House of Correction.

Fox was tried (by the same Nathaniel Barton whom he had preached against in All Saints and who was one of the Justices of the Peace for Derby at the time), and convicted of an offence under the newly introduced Blasphemy Act. He was sentenced to 6 months imprisonment but eventually served nearly a year, in appalling conditions, refusing to allow his relatives to stand surety for him. During this period Fox, in spite of his sufferings, was his usual contentious and obdurate self. His period of imprisonment in Derby was packed with incident. After a few weeks in prison he decided to write to the Ministers, Justices and Mayor who had had a part in sending him there. The tone of the letter can have done little to endear him to his persecutors. It read as follows:

> "I am forced in tender love unto your souls to write unto you, and to beseech you to consider what you do and what commands of God call for. He doth require justice and mercy, to break every yoke and to let the oppressed go free...consider what ye do in time, and take heed whom you imprison."[5]

Later, when his family arrived to arrange for his release, Fox was brought before the Justices again so that the amount of the suretyship could be decided. But he would not consent to this because, he says "I was innocent from any ill behaviour and had spoken the word of life and truth unto them". This so enraged Justice Gervase Bennett that, says Fox,

> "as I was kneeling down to pray to the Lord to forgive him, he ran upon me and struck me with both his hands crying 'away with him gaoler; take him away gaoler'...and some thought I was mad because I stood for purity, perfection and righteousness."[6]

All the while he continued to preach, dispute, argue and persuade anyone who cared to listen and a considerable number who did not. Eventually, as his original six month sentence was about to expire, he was invited, in an extraordinary tribute to his tenacity and leadership, to take a captaincy over a newly raised company of Derby troops. A meeting was arranged in the market place, but true to his pacifist principles, Fox declined and so irritated his opponents that the meeting was abruptly terminated. Fox relates:

> "Then their rage got up and they said 'Take him away gaoler and cast him into the dungeon amongst the rogues and felons' which they then did and put me into the dungeon amongst thirty felons in a lousy, stinking, low place in the ground without any bed."[7]

This was probably the prison in the Cornmarket. It had been constructed in 1588 and was built over a stream which, by 1650, was also the main town sewer. In 1645/6 it had been struck by plague and even without this additional hazard was clearly an exceedingly insanitary, uncomfortable and dangerous place to be.

The Derby authorities were clearly at a loss to know how to deal with a man like Fox, so in October 1651 he was finally released. His period in prison had obviously honed his opinions and strengthened his considerable powers of endurance. Fox viewed his incarceration as a sign of God's favour and by the following year he had embarked on his tour of Yorkshire and Lincolnshire, that established so many meeting houses and was to have a lasting influence on religious life in the northern counties.

He was never imprisoned in Derby again, although he managed to have himself arrested and imprisoned in Carlisle, Worcester, Leicester, Launceston and a number of other places along the way. He was a frequent visitor to the county, however, returning in 1652, 1654, 1655 and 1656 and 1658 and on numerous occasions after the Restoration up to 1680. On his visit to Derby in 1660, by a curious reversal of fate, he stayed with his former gaoler at the House of Correction, Thomas Sharman, who was now a converted Quaker.

There is no doubt that Fox's imprisonment in Derby was a turning point both for him and for Quakerism. It was his first lengthy spell in prison, it created considerable local interest at the time and he evidently made an impression on the people with whom he came into contact. Many of them were converted, and a substantial network of friends was established, particularly in Derby itself, and in the High Peak and Chesterfield areas. His dissenting views, largely apart from and unaffected by the institutional religious controversies of the age, evidently had more appeal for the common man than the dull bureaucracy of Presbyterianism; more emotional appeal, a greater sense of sharing and brotherhood, deepened by the persecution and imprisonment of many of the friends in Derbyshire and the surrounding counties. This is amusingly illustrated by the story told by Fox, of a Quaker woman in Chesterfield, Susan Frith. Blessed with the painful honesty of so many Quakers, she told the Chesterfield Justice, Clarke, that if he continued in his persecuting, the Lord would execute his plagues upon him. Shortly afterwards he went mad and "died distracted in chains".[8] The establishment and growth of Quakerism in the county laid the foundations for a long tradition of dissenting opinion for which Derbyshire is well known – a spirit of cussedness and local attachment that contributed in no small measure to the later growth of Methodism. For the convinced Presbyterian and the mystical Quaker these must have been times full of hope and promise; for the established church, however, they were difficult and turbulent.

The beginning of the end, in Derbyshire as elsewhere in the Midlands, was the ejecting of those Anglican vicars who were unsympathetic to the new order. Between 1644 and 1645, out of 108 benefices in the county, the vicars of 35 were ejected, more than 30 percent, while others followed in succeeding years, particularly 1652.[9] The evidence is still plain to see on the walls of parish churches from the High Peak to the Trent Valley; the lists of incumbents which Churches display, show an astonishing number of changes in the post Civil War period. At St Mary and All Saints

Chesterfield, for example, the Anglican William Edwards, Vicar since 1638 is dispossessed and replaced by the Puritan John Billingsley in 1653; at St Werburgh's Derby, the congregation chose an Independent Minister, Samuel Beresford and at Pentrich John Chapman was replaced by the Presbyterian Robert Pater, later to be prominent in the Wirksworth Classis; and the story was the same up and down the county.

The sufferings of these ordinary men, some of whom had faithfully served their parishes for decades, must have been very great. Ejectment meant not only the loss of income but also of home and friends. In addition, the county itself was relatively poor and had few rich livings. In the 1650 survey by the Committee for Plundered Ministers, out of 112 benefices in the county only 13 were worth more than £90 per year and 54 less than £39 per year, a poor reward even in those days. The situation of the poorer parishes was somewhat alleviated by Parliamentary grants (known as Augmentations) and by the mid 1650s the number of the poorest parishes had declined from 54 to 31 and the richest had increased to 16.[10] The survey of 1650, incidentally, gives an interesting and sometimes vivid portrait of the various Ministers in the county. "John Payne of Shirland – honest and able. Francis Talleme of Tibshelf – wicked and scandalous. Thomas Taylor of Sutton in the Dale – scandalous and hath been found in arms against the Parliament". Scandalous, of course, did not necessarily mean what it means today – it might merely be a comment on the individual's political allegiance.

On the restoration of the King, however, the boot was very much on the other foot; church ministers who were parliamentary supporters or, even worse, active republicans or Independents, could expect to be ejected as their Royalist predecessors had been. One of the earliest Acts passed by the Restoration Parliament required all Ministers ejected during the Interregnum to be reinstated by 25th December 1660, there being only two conditions, that they had not supported the execution of Charles I nor declared against infant baptism. Death, however, had taken a heavy toll of those who had originally been ejected in 1643 and 1644 and only three remained in the county, one of whom was Ezekial Coachman, the former vicar of Walton-on-Trent whose attempt to regain his parish from the then incumbent, Thomas Bearcroft, was to involve him in lengthy litigation.

Most parishes, therefore, continued to be occupied by Presbyterian or Independent ministers until the Act of Uniformity was passed in August 1662. This provided that the existing incumbents could retain their parishes, provided that they submitted to ordination by a Bishop (if they had not been so ordained) and accepted the Book of Common Prayer. The statistics of those who accepted and those who did not are an illuminating insight into the state of religious affairs in the county; 12 ordained ministers abjured their Presbyterian or Independent sympathies, adopted the Prayer Book and retained their benefices, including Emmanuel Bourne of Ashover, ever a man with an eye to his own position. A further 23 submitted to ordination, 15 resigned or died and 32 were ejected.[11] Considering the social and political pressures of the time, the number of Ministers who were prepared to lose all rather than submit to an Anglicanism in which they did not believe, indicates, I believe, the extent to which the county had been radicalised by its experiences during the war.

It should not be thought, incidentally, that Ministers of Religion in the county confined themselves purely to their religious duties. As has been mentioned above, at least one Royalist minister actually fought for the King and there were two prominent Parliamentarian supporters in the county as well; Captain Nathanial Barton was an officer in Gell's horse and the garrison commander at Barton House in 1643. He ultimately became a Colonel and took part in the Battles of Worcester and Preston. He was also a clergyman and the chaplain to Sir Thomas Burdett. His colleague Joseph Swetnam (or Swettenham) was the son of the vicar of St Alkmund's and was himself variously the Rector of Dalbury, Vicar of All Saints Derby and Rector of Whitwell. He was also a Captain of Horse under Gell, an active plotter during the Interregnum and took part in Booth's Rising of 1659. Such was the indivisible nature of politics and religion in seventeenth century England.[12]

12 Plots and Conspiracies

The miners are very numerous and have arms sufficient and hearts answerable to their resolutions.
The Levellers report support in Derbyshire.

The execution of the King in January 1649 set the seal on the triumph of the Independent party which now dominated the Parliament and the country. It also left a psychological void in the Royalist ranks that was difficult to fill and the few remaining embers of active Royalist resistance were snuffed out with relative ease.

The summer of 1649, however, was one of ferment up and down the country. There were mutinies in the Army over arrears of pay and the political future of the country and these disturbances were exploited by the Levellers, led by John Lilburne. The Levellers believed in complete equality and freedom for all and the abolition of all forms of political and religious hierarchy and in Derbyshire they found ready converts among the lead-miners of the Peak.

For some years past the miners had been in dispute with the Earl of Rutland over their right to sink mines wherever lead might be found, something that the Earl was unwilling to contemplate on his own personal estate (an early example of "not in my back-yard" perhaps?). The miners were backed by the local Leveller newspaper in Derby called The Moderate. On 8th September it reported "the miners are very numerous and have arms sufficient and hearts answerable to their resolutions" and that they would "maintain (a declaration of rights) with their lives and fortunes and likewise the Agreement of the People and the Petition of 11 September 1648",[1] a reference to the Leveller proposals for the reform of the constitution. Dissatisfied Cavaliers, always alert for an opportunity to embarrass the parliamentarian authorities, also supported the miners in their underground news-sheets.

The Government was clearly concerned about the threat of a revolt in Derbyshire over this issue, attendance at horse-racing, bowling and other public entertainments was forbidden but this did not deter the miners turning up in their thousands, many of them armed. On 10th October the Government ordered Thomas Sanders, now a Colonel in the New Model Army, to disperse, disarm and arrest them. This he did with efficiency and despatch and the revolt was over.

In August 1651, Charles II enlisted the somewhat unwilling help of the Scots and invaded England with an army. On 3rd September he met with the Parliamentary forces at Worcester and was heavily defeated; soon after he escaped to France and remained an exile until his restoration nine years later. Derbyshire was little involved in these events, although Thomas Sanders was involved with his Regiment at the Battle of Worcester and subsequently saw service with Cromwell in Scotland.

The defeat of the King at Worcester settled the affairs of England for a decade and Oliver Cromwell became the Protector of the English Republic. The leaden hand of the Major-Generals descended upon the county. In October of 1655 a proclamation appointed eleven Major Generals to rule over the country in the place of the old County Committees. Major-General Whalley was placed in charge of the associated counties of Lincoln, Nottingham, Derby, Warwick and Leicester. This did not deter Royalist conspirators from their plots, however. Throughout the period of Cromwell's rule, the Interregnum as it was later called, the country seethed with plots and conspiracies, in which almost every shade of opinion from High Anglicans to Fifth Monarchy men were involved. On the Royalist side, these were mainly hatched and co-ordinated, from the latter part of 1653, by a secret society called the Sealed Knot and there is no doubt that several members of the Derbyshire Royalist gentry were involved with it, and with its sister organization the Action Party. Their first large scale uprising was in March of 1655, the so-called Penruddock's Rising. The intention was to organize a national rising using the local Royalist associations and for months beforehand agents of the Sealed Knot were active in the Royalist areas and travelling to and fro between England and the Continent. Supplies of arms were sent to the local leaders under the guise of cases of wine, the recipient of one such being Edmund Browne of Bentley. In Derbyshire however the rising seems never to have got off the ground, although planning reached an advanced stage at nearby Staunton Harold, the home of a devoted Royalist Sir Robert Shirley; and at Rufford in Sherwood Forest there was a rendezvous of about 200 Royalists which broke up without anything being achieved.[2]

Plot and counter-plot, conspiracy and oppression continued for the whole of the Interregnum, the Royalists bedevilled at every turn by their own disunity and the efficiency of the secret service organised by Cromwell's Secretary of State, Thurloe. In August 1659, however, there was another attempt at national insurrection, Booth's Rising, in which Derbyshire was much more heavily involved.

The plans for the rising were co-ordinated by a new Royalist association, 'The Great Trust and Commission', or the Trust, as it was commonly known. In Derbyshire the leaders were Col. John Freschville and Philip Stanhope Earl of Chesterfield. Early in the morning of 12th August the Royalist conspirators in Nottinghamshire met in Sherwood Forest and attacked the local militia at Southwell who put up an unexpectedly strong resistance. The Royalists retreated and one of their leaders, Col. Charles

Colonel John Penruddock, leader of the Royalist Rising in 1655

From the author's collection

White, fled to Derby with a few men.

It appears that the preparations for the rising in Derby were well-advanced with a considerable degree of support from local Presbyterians particularly Robert Seddon of Kirk Langley and Luke Cranwell of Derby. On White's arrival a Declaration in favour of the King was read in the Market Place, "some crying a King, others a Free Parliament, some both". White was joined by a number of local shopkeepers and some of the militia officers. Col. Thomas Sanders made a half-hearted attempt to arrest the ringleaders but the mob prevented him. It is thought that he was in sympathy with the conspirators although he managed to avoid committing himself either way. Captain Samuel Doughty, the County Treasurer joined the rising, caused the bells to be rung to call in support from the countryside and, it is said, gave the rebels some £4,000 in recently collected taxes. Col. John Shalcross and Sir Henry Every raised a few supporters but the other Royalist leaders, including Freschville, apparently did nothing.

The Government was not slow in sending troops to crush the rising. By the afternoon of 12th August, Col. Mitchell arrived in Derby to warn the rebels that their conduct could not be tolerated and his troops entered the town without resistance on the following day. By 19th August, Booth's forces had been defeated in Cheshire and the rising was over.[3]

The end of the Interregnum was in sight, however. Oliver Cromwell had died in September of 1658 and had been replaced by his son, Richard, who lacked his father's firm hand. Parliament was dissolved and the country administered by a Council of Officers. But people were weary of the instabilities and oppressions of the Republic and, with Oliver Cromwell's death, a great deal of the personal devotion to him that had kept the Government in power, almost in spite of itself, ebbed away – the people were ready for a change, any change, even the restoration of the King.

In February 1660 General Monk, with his troops, entered London and was appointed Commander in Chief of the army. A new Parliament was convened and entered into negotiations with the King and on 25th May 1660 Charles II landed at Dover and travelled to London "amidst scenes of wild rejoicing" and, in the words of the old Cavalier song "The King enjoyed his own again".

In Derby, as elsewhere, the restoration of the monarchy was greeted with relief and celebration and, indeed, is still remembered in the county to this day in the ceremony of Oak Apple Day, 29th May, at Castleton. The bells of All Saints rang out when the King was proclaimed in Derby Market Place and the Constable of Repton rushed out to buy flags, drums and trumpets for the festivities.[4] In a very real sense, the Restoration was a much-needed national atonement for the execution of Charles I.

Epilogue

Let wise consider if this towne had been lost...what had become of neighbour counties, as also of Lankeshire and Cheshire.

Sir George Gresley on the importance of Derbyshire in the Civil War.

The restoration of the King brought a new era of peace and stability to the country and to Derbyshire, which took little time, it seems, to recover from the effects of eighteen years of war and uncertainty. By the 1660s the population of the county was probably over 60,000 and the traditional economic base of lead-mining would shortly be supplanted by some of the earliest sophisticated industrial processes, particularly the manufacture and weaving of silk. The Dutch looms for silk-weaving were, in fact, introduced by Thomas Cotchett, a barrister, who was born before the Civil War and was the son of the Robert Cotchett of Mickleover who witnessed the execution of the King.

For individuals, however, the scars did not heal so easily, and many of the principal players in the war had seen great changes in their fortunes. Sir John Gell disappears from our narrative in early 1646, disillusioned with the rise of the Independent party and, like many moderate Presbyterians, willing to come to an accommodation with the King. He also faced difficulties nearer at home; after the bitter in-fighting of the Recruiter Election, his old enemy Thomas Sanders laid charges against him of abuse of power and fraud and for many months he was involved in litigation with the Commons Committee of Privileges. He also attempted to recover the considerable (so he claimed) losses that he had sustained in the war and, to compound his difficulties, was also in disagreement with his wife over their complicated financial affairs.

After the execution of the King and his repeated failures in obtaining what he considered to be proper financial redress from Parliament, Gell had reason to be even more embittered and dissatisfied. In late December 1649 he was introduced to Colonel Eusebius Andrews, a Royalist barrister who had previously been an officer of the King's 1st Regiment. Andrews was concerned in a plot to attack and take the Isle of Ely to be used as a Royalist base to invade the country and he tried to involve Gell.[1] The true nature of Gell's involvement will never be known for sure, but it is clear that one of Andrew's associates, a Major John Bernard was probably an agent provocateur for the Parliament. At all events, Gell was arrested in the following March, and committed to the Tower, and his trial for High Treason began before the High Court of Justice on 11th September, 1650.

The evidence against him consisted largely of a letter which had supposedly been sent to him by Andrews but of which only a copy remained, Gell, apparently, having burnt the original. Upon this, and the testimony of some of his fellow conspirators, including his servant John Benson, Gell was convicted of misprision of treason and sentenced to life imprisonment. His estates were sequestrated but his lands in Derbyshire appear to have escaped forfeiture; the ever wily Gell had previously settled the lands on his son in return for an annuity, a device frequently resorted to during this period to

The tomb of Sir John Gell in Wirksworth Parish Church

Photo: D.J. Mitchell

keep lands and possessions in the family and to mitigate the effects of seizure and compounding. By 1652, however, his health was failing and he was released from prison. He was pardoned in 1653 and then lived in St Martin's Lane in London and took no further part in the affairs of the county. He died in 1671 and is buried at Wirksworth, where his tomb can still be seen in the parish church. The unfortunate Eusebius Andrews was not so lucky; he was executed.

The tomb of Colonel John Milward in St. Helen's Church, Darley Dale

Photo: D.J. Mitchell

Gell's brother Thomas (Sweet Tom Gell) was not so long-lived. He was elected MP for Derby a second time in 1652 and died unmarried in 1656.

Thomas Sanders of Little Ireton, Gell's old rival and bitter enemy, carved out a career for himself as a professional soldier in the New Model Army.[2] When the Derby Greycoats were disbanded in 1646 he took service with Colonel Thornaugh's Nottinghamshire Regiment and fought at Preston where Thornaugh was killed; Sanders succeeded him as Colonel and he was probably with his regiment at the Battle of Worcester in 1651. In 1654, however, he lost his commission for signing a petition against the dissolution of Parliament but was restored to his Colonelcy in 1659. He served as MP for Derby in 1654 and died a wealthy man at the ripe old age of 85 in 1695.

Of his contemporary Johannes Molanus, that faithful soldier and work-horse, we know little except that he was engaged in lead-smelting in 1655. His date of death is unknown.

On the Royalist side, William Cavendish, Duke of Newcastle, fled to Holland after the defeat of Marston Moor and lived in impecunious exile for many years returning only on the restoration of the King. He was able to rebuild his shattered estates, wrote a notable book on equitation and died full of honour and riches in 1676.

Philip Stanhope, Earl of Chesterfield was not so fortunate. Two of his sons were killed in the war, his estates were sequestrated and he died in 1656 in relative poverty.

The four "Country Colonels" who were the main support of Royalism in the county; Shallcross, Freschville, Milward and Eyre all had differing fates. Shallcross, as we have seen, remained an active Royalist to the last, and survived to see the restoration of the King, dying in 1673. Freschville was fortunate in his friendship with Parliamentarians, escaped substantial penalties during the Interregnum and was appointed Captain of Horse in the Royal Regiment in 1661. He became Baron Freschville of Staveley in 1664, served as MP for the county and died in 1682. John Milward of Snitterton compounded for his estates and was pardoned in 1646 and died in 1670 having served as MP for the County and written a most interesting diary of his term of office. Rowland Eyre of Hassop, as both a Catholic and a Royalist suffered harsher penalties; his estates were forfeit under the Treason Act of 1651 and he had eventually to re-purchase them for the enormous sum of £13,500. He died in 1674, and his family, like many Catholics, never really recovered from the financial strains of the conflict.[3]

Bibliography

As this bibliography is relatively short, and consists entirely of published material, I have not attempted to subdivide it into journal articles and books. Nor does it pretend to be in any way exhaustive; it is merely a list of books and articles that I have found helpful in writing this book. For those interested in pursuing further research into particular aspects of the Civil War in Derbyshire there is, of course, a large amount of manuscript material available at the Derby County Record Office at Matlock and also in private hands. For some of the latter, the reader is referred to the items in Trevor Brighton's excellent catalogue issued to accompany the Civil War Exhibition at Derby Museum in 1971 and which is included below.

ABBREVIATIONS

Clarendon	The History of the Rebellion and Civil Wars in England. Earl of Clarendon. Oxford 1849.
DAJ	Derbyshire Archaeological Journal.
DANHSJ	Journal of the Derbyshire Archaeological and Natural History Society.
DM	Derbyshire Miscellany.
EHR	English Historical Review.
Glover	History and Gazetteer of the County of Derby. Stephen Glover. 1829.
Hutchinson	Memoirs of the Life of Colonel Hutchinson. Lucy Hutchinson. Ed. C.H. Firth. 1906.
JBDHS	Journal of the Bakewell and District Historical Society.
Newcastle	The Life of William Cavendish, Duke of Newcastle. Margaret Cavendish. Ed. C.H. Firth. c. 1910.
TRHS	Transactions of the Royal Historical Society.
VCH	Victoria County History (Derbyshire).

Auden, Rev. A. M. Barton Blount in the Civil War DANHSJ Vol 43 1921

Barker, S. A. Civil War and Civil Strife in South West Derbyshire 1500–1650 DM Vol 9 1982

Brailsford, H. N. The Levellers and the English Revolution (Ed. C. Hill) 1983

Brighton, J. T. Royalists and Roundheads in Derbyshire. JBDHS 1981

Brighton, J. T. The Gell Family in the Sixteenth and Seventeenth Centuries. JBDHS 1980

Brighton, J. T. Sir John Gell and the Civil War in Derbyshire. JBDHS 1981

Brighton, J. T. Sir John Gell Governor of Derby 1642–46. JBDHS 1982

Brighton, J. T. Derby and the Civil War (Museum Catalogue) 1971

Clarendon, Edw. Hyde Earl of, The History of the Rebellion and Civil Wars in England 1849, 7 Vols.
Clayton, H. Loyal and Ancient City – the Civil War in Lichfield n.d.
Cotchett, R. A letter relating to the execution of the King – reproduced in DANHSJ Vol 72, 1952
Cox, J. C.(Ed.) The Minute Book of the Wirksworth Classis, DANHSJ, Vol 2, 1890
Cox, J. C. Three Centuries of Derbyshire Annals 1890
Cox, J. C. The Chronicles of the Collegiate Church or Free Chapel of All Saints, Derby 1881
Cox, J. C.(Ed.) Proceedings of the Derbyshire Committee for Compounding and other Commonwealth Papers DANHSJ Vol 13 1891
Cox, J. C. Documents relative to the sequestration of the Derbyshire Estates of Philip First Earl of Chesterfield. DANHSJ Vol 11. 1889
Dias, J. R. Lead, Society and Politics in Derbyshire before the Civil War. Midland History 1981
Dore, R. N.(Ed.) The Letter Books of Sir William Brereton, 1984
Edwards, D. G. Population in Derbyshire in the Reign of King Charles II. DAJ 1982
Farmer, Rev. R. L. A Cavalier's Sword Found at Egginton DANHSJ, Vol 27, 1905
Firth, C. H. Cromwell's Army, 1967
Fisher, F. N. The Civil War Papers of the Constable of Hope DANHSJ, Vol 70, 1950
Fisher, F. N. The Every Family and the Civil War DANHSJ, Vol 74, 1954
Fletcher, A. The Outbreak of the English Civil War 1981
Fletcher, A. J. Petitioning and the Outbreak of the Civil War in Derbyshire. DAJ Vol 93, 1973
Fox, G. Journal of George Fox (Ed. J. L. Nichalls) 1975
Glover, S. History and Gazetteer of the County of Derby 1829
Hensman, E. W. The East Midlands and the Second Civil War. TRHS, 4th Series, Vol 6, 1923
Hutchinson, Lucy. Memoirs of Colonel Hutchinson (Ed. by C. H. Firth) 1906
Hutton, W. The History of Derby, 1791
Kirkham, N. Wingfield Manor in the Civil War DM Vol 6, 1973
Kirkham, N. The Leeke Family in the Civil War DM Vol 7, Pt I 1974
Kirkham, N. Royalist Conspiracies and Derbyshire DM Vol 7 Pt II 1974
Newcastle, Margaret Duchess of. Memoirs of the Duke of Newcastle (Ed. C. H. Firth) nd c.1910
Newton, S. C. The Gentry of Derbyshire in the Seventeenth Century, DAJ Vol 86, 1966
Pendleton, J. History of Derbyshire, 1966
Sherwood, R. G. Civil Strife in the Midlands 1642–51 1974
Sitwell, Sir G. The Derbyshire Petition of 1641. DANHSJ. Vol 19, 1897
Symonds, R. The Complete Military Diary (Ed. by S. Peachey) 1989
Tibbutt, H. G. (Ed) The Letter Books of Sir Samuel Luke 1644–45. HMSO 1963
Turbutt, G. A History of Ogston. 1975

Underdown, D. Party Management in the Recruiter Elections EHR, Vol 83, 1968
Underdown, D. Royalist Conspiracy in England 1649–1660. 1960
Wood, A. C. Nottinghamshire in the Civil War 1971
Young, P. Newark-on-Trent – the Civil War Siegeworks, HMSO 1964
Young, P. & Holmes, R. The English Civil War, 1974
Young, P. Marston Moor 1644. 1970

Notes

Notes, arranged by Chapters.

As both the Gell and the Gresley manuscripts are reprinted in full as an Appendix, the numerous quotations from them are not included in these Notes.

CHAPTER 1

1. I have relied for these figures largely on the Victoria County History of Derbyshire, Vol. II p. 184. The interested reader might also usefully consult D.G. Edwards' article, "Population in Derbyshire in the Reign of Charles II; the use of Hearth Tax Assessments and the Compton Census". DAJ 1982 p. 106 et seq.
2. "Lead, Society and Politics in Derbyshire before the Civil War" by Jill R. Dias in Midland History 1981, Vol. VI p. 39 to p. 57. This was invaluable for the factual aspects of lead mining. Much useful material may also be found in VCH Vol. II, p. 357.
3. Readers interested in curious legal survivals may wish to know that the Barmote Court still sits annually and a special clay pipe or 'churchwarden' is presented to each member. Its other functions are unclear!
4. VCH Vol. II p. 181 et seq.
5. W.A. Richardson "A Citizen's Derby". p. 91.
6. For transport generally see Drury "The East Midlands and the Peak" p. 89, and "Nottingham and its Region". Ed. K.C. Edwards, p. 316.
7. VCH Vol. II pp. 182 and 183.
8. Dias, op. cit.
9. Dias, op. cit.
10. J.C. Cox. "Three Centuries of Derbyshire Annals". Vol. 1 p. 290.
11. J.T. Brighton. "Royalists and Roundheads in Derbyshire". See also S.C. Newton "The Gentry of Derbyshire in the Seventeenth Century". DAJ Vol. 86. 1966.

CHAPTER 2

1. J.C. Cox. "Annals". Vol. II p. 107.
2. J.C. Cox. "Annals". Vol. II p. 110 et seq.
3. Hutchinson. p. 101.
4. J.T. Brighton. "The Gell Family in the Sixteenth and Seventeenth Centuries". p. 12.
5. See generally A.J. Fletcher "The Outbreak of the English Civil War" particularly p. 382.
6. A.J. Fletcher. "Petitioning and the Outbreak of the Civil War in Derbyshire". DAJ Vol. 93. 1973. p. 34 et seq.

7. Quoted in A.J. Fletcher op. cit. p. 35.
8. A.J. Fletcher op. cit. p. 36.
9. A.J. Fletcher op. cit. p. 37.

CHAPTER 3

1. Hutchinson. pp. 101 and 102.
2. See A.J. Fletcher op. cit.
3. A. Everitt "The Community of Kent and the Great Rebellion." Leicester University Press. 1973.
4. See J.T. Brighton "Royalists and Roundheads" and Newton "The Gentry of Derbyshire".
5. Clarendon Vol. II pp. 359 and 360.
6. Clarendon Vol. II p. 320.
7. Glover Vol. 1 p. 76 (Appendix)
8. A caliver was an early variety of matchlock firearm, by this time obsolescent if not obsolete.
9. A musket was its successor, heavier in weight, firing a heavier bullet to a greater range and normally used with a forked rest to support the barrel.
10. A saker was an artillery piece, firing a ball of about 5¼ lbs weight to a range of some 1200 yards.
11. The term 'horse' was commonly used to mean cavalry; as 'foot' meant infantry.

CHAPTER 4

1. Hutchinson p. 116.
2. A drake is usually understood to mean a shorter and lighter version of an artillery piece, with a shorter range; e.g. a cannon drake, or a culverin drake.
3. The term 'reformado' was normally used to mean a gentleman volunteer or ranker.
4. Clarendon Vol. II pp. 518 and 519.
5. I have relied heavily for this account of the battle on J.T. Brighton's illuminating and well-researched narrative in Vol. VIII of the Journal of the Bakewell and District Historical Society.

CHAPTER 5

1. Hutchinson. p. 403.
2. Meant here in the technical sense of an artillery piece firing a heavy ball of about 47 lbs to a range of some 2000 yards.
3. Hutchinson. p. 144.
4. See Gell's Account in Appendix; and Hutchinson, p. 150 et seq.

CHAPTER 6

1. Newcastle. p. 32.
2. Newcastle. p. 32, footnote 1.
3. Hutchinson. p. 408.
4. Newcastle. p. 197.

CHAPTER 7

1. Hutchinson. pp 423 and 424.
2. See Hutchinson. p. 175 et seq.
3. See Rev. R.L. Farmer "A Cavalier's Sword found at Egginton." DANHSJ Vol. 27. 1905.
4. Quoted in P. Young. "Marston Moor 1644". p. 55.
5. For the position and strength of the Derbyshire forces I have relied on P. Young. op. cit.
6. Apart from Gell's Account see also N. Kirkham "Wingfield Manor in the Civil War" in DM Vol. VI. Pt. 5.
7. A type of earthen artillery fortification.
8. For Barton Blount generally see A.M. Auden "Barton Blount and the Civil War" in DANHSJ Vol. 43. 1921.

CHAPTER 8

1. Quoted in J.T. Brighton "Sir John Gell, Governor of Derby 1642–46" in the Journal of the Bakewell and District Historical Society. Vol. 9. Jan. 1982 p. 4. For much of this chapter and Chapter 9 I am indebted to his pioneering work.
2. J.T. Brighton op. cit. p. 30.
3. J.T. Brighton op. cit. p. 30.
4. For those who may be interested in the more obscure byways of history, the original of the astrological prediction is in the Bodleian Library, Ashmole MS 184.
5. Grenades or granadoes were used in the assault, a fairly rare instance in the Midland Counties. Some of the originals have been identified by staff at the Newarke Houses Museum in Leicester. They were spherical pots, with a fuse at the top, and were filled with gunpowder, saltpetre, sulphur, hog's grease, pitch, alcohol and sal ammoniac, a sort of early napalm.
6. Quoted in Firth "Cromwell's Army" p. 316.
7. See A.C. Wood "Nottinghamshire in the Civil War". p. 103 et seq.

CHAPTER 9

1. See J.T. Brighton "Sir John Gell and the Derby Committee" in the Journal of the Bakewell and District Historical Society Vol. IX p. 31 et seq. Also D. Underdown "Party Management in the Recruiter Elections" EHR Vol. 83.
2. Who later witnessed the execution of King Charles (Note 8.)
3. J.T. Brighton op. cit. p. 33.
4. J.T. Brighton op. cit. p. 39.
5. Glover Vol. I. p. 82. (Appendix.)
6. Quoted in J. Pendleton "History of Derbyshire". p. 278. It was referred to in a letter from Emmanuel Bourne of Ashover to his cousin, William Bourne. See also Note 17, Chapter 10.
7. Quoted in R.E. Sherwood "Civil Strife in the Midlands 1642–51" p. 222.
8. See DANHSJ Vol. 72. p. 131 et seq.
9. N. Kirkham "The Leeke Family in the Civil War". DM Vol. VII. Pt. I. p. 1.

CHAPTER 10

1. J.T. Brighton "Royalists and Roundheads". pp. 77 and 78.

2. Quoted in Hutchinson. p. 396.
3. Glover Vol. I. p. 75.
4. "The Letter Books of Sir Samuel Luke 1644–45". Ed. H.G. Tibbutt. p. 170. HMSO.
5. F.N. Fisher. "The Civil War Papers of the Constables of Hope". DANHSJ Vol. 70. p. 73.
6. Fisher op. cit. p. 75.
7. C. Carlton in "The impact of the English Civil War". Ed. J. Morrill. p. 20. Actually the figure is an extraordinarily precise one of 84,738 which I have rounded up.
8. "Richard Symonds – the Complete Military Diary". Ed. Stuart Peachey. p. 62.
9. J.C. Cox "Chronicles of All Saints, Derby". p. 206.
10. Rev. A.M. Auden "Barton Blount and the Civil War". DANHSJ Vol. XLIII. p. 14.
11. Auden op. cit. p. 14 et seq.
12. See J.C. Cox "Proceedings of the Derbyshire Committee for Compounding". DANHSJ Vol. 13; J.C. Cox "Documents Relative to the Sequestration of the Derbyshire Estates of Philip, First Earl of Chesterfield". DANHSJ Vol. 11; and F.N. Fisher "The Every Family and the Civil War". DANHSJ Vol. 74.
13. Newcastle. p. 73 et seq.
14. Glover Vol. I. p. 84.
15. Newcastle. p. 79.
16. J.C. Cox "Derbyshire Annals" Vol. I. p. 163.
17. Pendleton op. cit. p. 271 et seq.

CHAPTER 11

1. The Papal pronouncement of 1570 which declared Elizabeth a heretic and a bastard, and absolved all Catholics from their allegiance to her.
2. See J.C. Cox (Ed.) "The Minute Book of the Wirksworth Classis" in DANHSJ Vol. 2. p. 135 et seq.
3. Cox op. cit. p. 157.
4. Cox op. cit. p. 158.
5. Journal of George Fox. Ed. John L. Nickalls. Society of Friends. 1975. p. 54.
6. Nickalls op. cit. p. 61.
7. Nickalls op. cit. p. 65.
8. Nickalls op. cit. p. 509.
9. J.C. Cox "Derbyshire Annals". Vol. I. p. 320.
10. "A Good and Sufficient Maintenance – the Augmentation of Parish Livings in Derbyshire 1645–60". DAJ 1980. p. 69 et seq.
11. VCH Vol. II p. 31.
12. See Brighton "Royalists and Roundheads" p. 45 for a summary of the life and career of this interesting priest.

CHAPTER 12

1. H.N. Brailsford "The Levellers and the English Revolution". p. 567.
2. D. Underdown. "Royalist Conspiracy in England".
3. D. Underdown. op. cit. p. 276 et seq.
4. W.A. Richardson. "A Citizen's Derby". p. 106.

EPILOGUE

1. See Underdown and also N. Kirkham "Royalist Conspiracies and Derbyshire Part I" in DM Vol. VII. p. 55 et seq. Unfortunately Nellie Kirkham did not live to complete Part II.
2. As to which, see Firth "The Later History of the Ironsides" in TRHS N.S. Vol. 15.
3. I have always found that one of the most irritating aspects of a general history like this is that it never tells you what happened in later years to the various minor characters! For those who wish to find out, I recommend the excellent potted biographies in Trevor Brighton's "Royalists and Roundheads".

Appendix

There are three local contemporary accounts of the Civil War in Derbyshire, one written by Sir John Gell himself, and shorter versions written by his brother Thomas and by Gell's friend and supporter Sir George Gresley. The first and last were printed in Glover's History and Gazeteer of the County of Derby in 1829 and have not, to my knowledge, been re-printed since, except for an annotated version of Gell's narrative recently produced by a specialist firm of Civil War publishers and having only limited circulation. It seemed appropriate, therefore, to re-print both accounts here in the hope that they might reach a wider audience. A word or two of caution, however; it should be borne in mind that both accounts were written in support of Gell's claim to Parliament for his alleged arrears of pay and expenses incurred on their behalf in the First Civil War. It should be expected, therefore, that they will put the best construction on his actions, playing down any discreditable areas and exaggerating, where it might serve his purposes, the help and support that he gave. Nevertheless, the accounts are, in my view, worth reproducing here if only for their vivid and sometimes racy language, and for the fact that they are the only substantial contemporary accounts of the war in and around the county that are now available to us. I have used them with caution in writing this book and, wherever possible, have checked their accuracy against other accounts in *The Life of Colonel Hutchinson*, *Memoirs of the Duke of Newcastle* and other contemporary material. The reader may assume, however, that the dates and sequence of events is generally correct.

Gell's Account

A true relation of what Service hath beene done by Colonell Sir John Gell, Bart. for the Kinge and the Parliament, in Defence of the Towne and County of Derby, and how ayding and assisting hee hath beene to the adjacent Countyes, viz. Nottinghamshire, Staffordshire, Cheshire Lancashire, Lincolnshire and Yorkshire, from October, 1642, till October, 1646

The 11th of October, 1642, the above named Colonell Sir John Gell had a company of ffoot from Hull, contayning one hundred and forty. The 16th of the said moneth hee marched with his sayd company to Wheatfield, where the souldyers their mutined, but, by the intreaty of Capt. Bright, now Col. Bright, and the minister of the towne, many of them were disarmed, and the remainder sett in good posture. The 17th hee marched to Chesterfield, and their remayned eight or nine dayes, where hee raysed by the beate of a drum, two hundred men, some with arms and some without. The 26th hee marched to Wirksworth, where Sir Ffrancis Wortley, with his rebel rout, hearing of his approach, fled away, but there Colonell Gell remayned three or four days, and increased his fforces to three hundred and above. And so the 31st of October 1642, hee marched to Derby towne, and theire hee began to give out comyshons for his officers. Some five dayes after Captayne White came to him out of Nottinghamshire, with a company of dragoones, consisting of about twenty-seven, but before hee departed hee made them upp one hundred and forty, all well armed, under the command of the said Sir John Gell. About the 10th of November, 1642, the aforesaid Sir Ffrancis Wortley returned againe to the towne of Dale, in Derbyshire, whither Sir John, mounted his musquetiers and forced him out of the countrey. The 25th of November, having his regiment compleate, hee horsed about three hundred musquetiers with Captayne White's dragoones, and sent them by Major Mollanus to Coventrey for two saccers and some ammunition; when they came thither, they kept them five dayes their, because they had intelligence that the enemy were approaching towards the city. As soon as they returned to Derby Colonell Gell, having intelligence that the Earl of Chesterfield had fortified his house with forty musquetiers, horse and seven drakes, whereupon hee commanded forth of Derby some four hundred fforth, and Captayne White's dragoones and two sakers to the said Earle's house, called Bratby, Major Mollanus being commander in chiefe. Uppon the approach of our men, the enemy shott their drakes and musketts at them; but after halfe a dozen shotts of our saccers and musquetiers, and our men beginning to fall upon their workes, the said Earl with all his fforces ffled away through his parke and so to Litchfield. Wee, forsably entring the house, found his Countess, her gentlewoman and two or three servants therein, seized presently upon the armes, and found seven drakes, thirty steele pikes, twenty or thirty musquetts, five double barrells of powder and good store of match and bulletts. Major Mollanus, Captayne White, Captayne Sanders and divers other officers entreated the Countess that shee would give every souldyer halfe a crowne, for to have her house saved from plundering, because it was a free boottey. She answered, it was too much, and that she had not so much monyes; they asked her againe if shee would give amongst them forty marks: shee made the same answer, that shee had not monyes. Then they offered to deposit the money for her, if shee would promise to repay it them: she still refractoroly and willfully said, that shee would not give them one penny; and then indeed the souldyers plundred the house. But the said officers saved her owne chamber, with all the goods therein. Then Derbyshire being cleared, Captayne White went to Nottingham Castle, seized uppon all the arms, and sent to Sir John Gell immediately to assist him, with some ffoott, whereuppon hee sent his Major Mollanus with three hundred ffoott, when he began to fortefie Nottingham and sett them in a posture of defense, and assisted Colonell Peirpoynt to make up his regiment of ffoott, and we continued their some nine or ten dayes, in the intervale Sir John Gell having intelligence that Colonell Hastings was come to Ashby-de-la-Zouch with three hundred horse and four hundred ffoott, and still raysing as many as hee could, sent for the said Major Mollanus with his three hundred ffoott back againe to Derby, and by that tyme Hastings was fortefiing Sir John Harpur's house and Swarkeston bridge, whereuppon hee prepared his whole regiment with Sir George Gresley's troope of horse, which hee had raysed since Captayne White went from Derby to Nottinghamshire, and soe having two saccers along with him hee marched thither, stormed their works, drove the enemy away, and dismantled the same, killed seven or eight of them and wounded many, and but one man of his wounded, soe that the enemy never had a mind to fortifie the same againe. He was no sooner returned to Derby, but the moorlanders in Staffordshire came to him, entreating him for assistance, because the enemy had possessed themselves in Stafford towne. Sir John asked them what assistance they would have; they said two hundred musquetiers and one saccer, not doubting but that they had men enough, with that assistance to regayne the town, and to save themselves. Hee commanded his said Major Mollanus immediately with two hundred ffoott and one saccer to march towards their appointed rendezvouz, att Uttoxeter. His Major being their two or three dayes, and nobody coming to assist him, and hearing that the enemy increased, was forced to retreate in the night to Derby, being vi. long miles: in the meane tyme Colonell Hastings strongly fortefyed Ashby-de-la-Zouch, which was, and would be, a great hinderance to Leicestershire, Staffordshire and Derbyshire. My Lord Grey sent to him, that hee should make ready with all the forces he could make, and that Sir William Brereton was likewise to meete him with some forty horse, to goe against the said Ashby, within two dayes after hee mett my Lord Grey with all the strengh hee had, and joyning their fforces togeather, they marched to the said Ashby, where they found the towne fortefyed, assaulted it, and beate the enemy into the mansion-house, with the loss of four or five men of our side, and one leiftennant of ffoott of ours wounded; and having gotten the towne, wee planted our ordnance against the mansion-house, but before they could doe any execution, their was a letter brought to my Lord Grey from the committee of Northampton, how that Prince Rupert was marched from Banbury to come to relieve the said Ashby, whereuppon my Lord called a councell of warr, and by the said councell it was agreed, that they should drawe off, finding themselves too weake.

February 24th, 1643, by an order from his excellence, the late Earl of Essex, he was commanded to send what strength hee could well spare under the command of Major-Generall Ballard against Newarke, whereuppon he sent Major Mollanus with five hundred ffoott, because one ffoott company of his regiment, under Captayne Mundy, was commanded to Yorkshire, Captayne Stafford with his ffoot company at Whalybridge uppon the borders of Lancashire and Cheshire, and his said Major's owne ffoott company at Burton uppon Trent, and left in Derby only Captayne Mellor's ffoott company, and Sir George Gresley's troope to defend the towne. Whilest these his fforces were soe abroad, and himself att Derby, their came news to him, how my Lord Brooks had entered Litchfield and beseidged the closе, who, by reviewing the workes, was their unfortunately slayne, and presently after his death, my said Lord officers made choyse of Colonell Gell to bee their commander in cheife for the present service. Hee went immediately with Sir George Gresley's troopes to Litchfield, and approached to the close with our morterpeece as neare as possably hee could, and after hee had shott three granadees they fell to parlee and surrendered the close and themselves prisoners unto him. In the meane tyme the said Major Mollanus returned with his ffoott from Newarke, and came to him at Litchfield, and soe Colonell Gell, asking him howe they had prospered before Newarke, he answered that he redily thought they were betrayed by the commander in cheife, which was Major-Generall Ballard, for that they had entred the towne and mastred the workes, and then commanded back, by the said Ballard, without doing any thinge att all, and soe returned with the losse of some men and one drake, and had nott Nottingham men and his stood against the said Ballard's will, closely one to another, they had lost all their ordnance, which they fetched off, whether hee would or not. And when hee had gayned Litchfield cloase, and sett all in good order, Sir William Brereton sent him a letter to meete him at Hopton Heath, near Stafford, with all the strengh hee could make, to goe against Stafford towne, and soe they marched togeather towards Hopton Heath, where Colonell Gell commanded all the ffoott, and Sir William Brereton the horse; presently they descryed the enemy, whereuppon hee sett his ffoott in order of battalis, and Sir William his horse, the enemy advancing in a full body with above one thousand two hundred horse, whereof the Earl of Northampton was generall, and soe setting upon their horse, Sir William's horse presently rann away, and left Sir John Gell alone with the ffoot. The enemy drew his horse into a body againe, and charged his ffoott, but he gave them such a salute, that the enemy, in a disordered manner, drew off and marched away towards Stafford, but left many dead bodies behind them, whereof my Lord of Northampton was one, Captyne Middleton and many other brave commanders of horse and at least one hundred dragoones; and of our side three carters and two souldyers were slayne, we lost two caskes of drakes, which the dragoones had drawne a great distance from the ffoott, under the hedges to save themselves, and soe Colonell Gell retreated with my Lord's dead body towards Uttoxeter, with his fforces, and Sir William Brereton with his fforces towards Cheshire. And att Uttoxeter Colonell Gell remayned three dayes, and sett Staffordshire in as good posture as hee could; within the said three dayes their came a trumpetter to him from my younge Lord of Northampton, for his father's dead body, whereuppon hee answered, if hee would send him the drakes which they had gotten from their dragoones and pay the chiurgeons for embalming it, hee should have it: but hee returned him an answer, that hee would doe neither th' one nor th' other, and soe Colonell Gell caused him to be carried in his company to Derby, and buried him in the Earle of Devonshire's sepulcher in All Hallowes church. April 8th, 1643, Colonell Chadwicke having gotten some three hundred of Yorkshire and Scarsdales horse togeather, sent word to Colonell Gell that my Lord of Deincourt did usually send assistance to Boulsouer, and was fortefying his own house, hee, in all the haste hee could, sent his Leiftennant Colonell, Thomas Gell, and his Major with five hundred men and three peeces of ordnance to the said Lord Deincourt's house; and att their coming my Lord stood uppon his defence, but in the conclusion Leiftennant Colonell Gell tooke the house, and my Lord and all his fforces, with the loss of two or three men of our side. My Lord promised faithfully uppon his honor to come within eight dayes next after to Derby, and submitt himselfe to the Parliament's censure, but Leiftennant Colonell Gell demolished the workes which were about the house, and soe retreated to Derby, but hee was no sooner marched away, but my Lord went to Newarke, and never came to Derby, for all his honor, promises and protestations.

Presently after Colonell Gell sent to my Lord Grey, desiring his assistance for the taking of Burton, by reason it was the only passage over the Trent and Dove into the North. My Lord within two dayes came, and mett Colonell Gell att the rendezvouse, on Egginton Heath, and soe marched togeather to the said Burton, drove the enemy away, and Colonell Gell left one of his bigest ffoott companys their, consisting of two hundred, under Captayne Sanders, and one peece of ordnance, and presently after made sixty dragoones, and soe kept the passage.

About the beginning of May, 1643, their came a command from my said Lord Grey, that Colonell Gell should march with all his fforces and attillery and meete at the randezvouze att Nottingham, and soe uppon my Lord's command Colonell Gell marched thither with all his fforces and attillery, excepting one ffoott company, and their wee were put under the command of Younge Hotham, where then were present my said Lord Grey with his fforces, Colonell Cromwell with his fforces, and all Nottingham fforces, soe that in all wee were about five or six thousand horse and ffoott but the greatest parte of horse, and marched upp and down in the vale of Belvour for the space of one moneth till the Queene came to Newarke with great strength, and then my Lord Grey retreated towards Leicester, Cromwell towards Peterborrough, Colonell Hubbard with his regiment tarried at Nottingham, under the command of Sir John Meldrum, and Colonell Gell to Derby, because they conceived they were not able to encounter with the enemy for want of ffoott.

In the meane tyme that wee left Captayne Sanders at Burton, one Mr. Houghton, a Lancashire man, was made Colonell, and hee made the said Sanders his Leiftennant Colonell, soe that Colonell Gell lost that great company and above sixty dragoones horse and armes, which was a great losse to Derbyshire when the enemy were soe aboute us. The Queene being att Newarke, and understanding that wee were all soe dispersed, marched with her fforces towards Ashby-de-la-Zouch: Colonell Gell having true intelligence that shee was marching westwards, and that shee would fall uppon Burton, because it was the chiefe passage from South to the North, sent presently to Staffordshire for all the fforces to meete him, and likewise to Nottingham, where were about three thousand horse and ffoott, and hee himselfe would draw out with all his fforces to Egginton Heath, and soe to Burton, to assist them till the Queene were past, but noebody would come, soe that within three days after shee marched towards Burton, tooke the towne by storme, killed many of them, tooke the Colonell, Leiftennant Colonell, and most of the officers prisoners, and soe most miserably plundered and destroyed the towne.

The Queene was noe sooner departed out of Staffordshire but the countrey men sent to Colonell Gell, how that Sir Richard Ffleetwood had fortefyed his house, and encreased very strong both in horse and ffoott, and did great hurt in plundering the traffique betwixt Lancashire, Cheshire and Derby, by robbing and stopping of carriers, which went weekly from

Manchester to London, hee sent presently his Lieftennant Colonell with about four hundred ffoott and one troope of horse to the said Ffleetwood's house, and tooke it by storme, and brought Sir Richard prisoner to Derby, with all his men, being betwixt seventy and eighty.

Within five weeks after Colonell Gell having intelligence how that Hastings was fallen out with one Raggard, governor of Litchfield, and departed from thence with such fforces as hee had to Tutbury, and their devoured all the provision they had; and that if Colonell Gell would come and besedge it for four dayes, with considerable strength, they must needs surrender it for want of victualls and ammunition, and by that meanes hee might release most of the prisoners taken at Burton, whereof Colonell Houghton was one. Uppon this intelligence Colonell Gell sent to Sir John Meldrum, at Nottingham, for assistance: Sir John Meldrum came presently to Derby, with Major Ireton, and Captayne White, with some two hundred horse and dragoones, and soe Colonell Gell marched along with them with all his fforces, horse and ffoott, and artillery to Tutbury towne, and surrounded the castle; their wee remayned two dayes and one night. Sir John Meldrum calling a councell of war, tould them how hee had intelligence that the Earl of Newcastle was sending fforces to relieve it out of Yorkshire and Bridge North, whereuppon it was resolved that wee should retreat to severall garrisons. Soe soon as Sir John Meldrum came to Nottingham, hee drewe all the fforces then in towne, excepting some four hundred, which hee left in the castle with Colonell Hutchinson, and marched southwards towards Peterborrough; but Nottingham townsmen sent for ayde to Colonell Gell to assist them, while they were removing their goods into the castle, for they were left in a most miserable condition: hee presently made ready three hundred dragoones and sent thither his said Major Mollanus, to continue there till they had moved their goods into the castle, and left the towne desolate, but some few of the townsmen within; awhile after newes came that the enemy had entred the towne, and had beseiged the castle, the Governor with the Committee, did most earnestly send unto Colonell Gell, that hee should with all speede send them assistance, otherwise the castle would be taken, because most of their souldyers were in the towne, and many an honest man would soe be starved, who had privily hid themselves. Sir John presently made ready all the strength hee could, and gott together all the horses in the countrey, and horsed some five hundred musquetiers, with the assistance of two or three troopes at Leicester, and soe with all that strength marched to Nottingham, Major Mollanus being commander in chiefe. The enemy was then at least five or six hundred in Nottingham towne, horse and ffoott, and stood all in battalio in the market-place, and all our fforces were not five hundred. The said Major Mollanus with Captayne Hacker, now Colonell Hacker, entred the towne with their horse, were presently beaten backe, lost four or five horses, instantly after the said Major broke thorrow the enemy and brought in the dragoones, and entred the towne againe, and drove the enemy before them, many of them slayne, and one hundred and sixty taken prisoners, but one man of our side slayne, which was namely one Captayne Leiftennant Lenerick, who led Colonell Gell's owne troope, three men wounded, and some five or six horses killed. Wee releived at the same tyme at least four hundred townsmen and souldyers of the castle, who were almost famished. The remainder of the enemy fled to Nottingham bridge, which they were then fortefying.

Within tenn dayes after, the Committee of Nottingham sent again unto Colonell Gell, that hee might needs send them present ayde and assistance to beate the enemy from the bridge, otherwise they would bee soe restrayned that they would not be able to keepe the castle; the enemy possessing the bridge, the castle was to noe effect; Colonell Gell presently commanded between three and four hundred horse and dragoones to march to Nottingham and assist them, whereof Major Mollanus was cheif commander; and thither went, and drove the enemy away, soe that it will be adgudged by any councell of warr, that Nottingham towne and castle had been long since in the enemy's possession, had they not had the assistance of Sir John Gell in driving the enemy from them at *every* tyme of neede, as the Colonells and Committee of Nottinghamshire did ever acknowledge.

Within a while after, Colonell Gell had intelligence that Sir Thomas Ffairefax was come to Nottingham with two thousand horse; hee went thither to see him, and soe Sir Thomas Ffairefax tould him that hee must goe to Wingfield Manor to communicate with some Derbyshire gentlemen, whereof one was Mr. Milward, which had beene a Captayne of the trayned band, to persuade him to take upp armes for the parliament: but it was too late, because hee had before taken Commission of the Kinge for a regiment of ffoott, as since it most apparently appeared. And this was tould Sir Thomas before, but hee would not believe it, but since hee found it to bee true; soone after Sir Thomas repaired to Derby with all his horse,and their continued for two or three dayes, and desired of Colonell Gell that hee would lett him have four or five hundred musquetiers to march with him towards Chesterfield, and from thence to Yorkshire; whereuppon he answered, that hee had not about five hundred men in Derby to defend the towne, and that Hastings had at that tyme at least two thousand at Litchfield, Ashby-de-la-Zouch and Tutbury, still looking for ann opportunity to surprise Derby, if his horses had marched out of it; because it was well knowne, that if Derby were taken, Nottingam could not long hold out, and then all the north side of Trente was lost. Nevertheless Colonell Gell tould him, that hee had one hundred men at Wingfield Mannor, whereof hee should have sixty; and Captain Taylor's Company, which was at Wingerworth, much about the same number; and of Captain Stafford's Company, who were at Chatesworth, forty; and Captain

Hadfield's Company, to make them upp four hundred, wherewith he was well pleased, and soe marched towards Chesterfield, whereat came to him one hundred and twenty musquetiers of the number aforesaid.

Sir John Gell and the Committee ordered that Leiftennant Colonell and Mr. Hallowes, two of the said Committee, should repaire to Chesterfield for to provide such things as were necessary for Sir Thomas Ffairefax and his horses. As soone as they came thither, they had an allaram that the Earl of Newcastle, with all the fforces, were marching towards Derbyshire; whereuppon Sir Thomas gave orders, that his horse should retreat to Nottingham and willed the two Committees to shift for themselves; and that this was noe countrey hee could defend with his fforces, and soe hee left us, and went cleare away towards Leicestershire, whither Colonell Gell and the Committees did often write unto him; yea, and sent two of the Committee to intreate him to come and assist them, and that the Earl of Newcastle's fforces were not above two thousand at that instant in Derbyshire, with whom Colonell Gell could well deale, if hee had come in any tyme. Upon this hee made many promises, not only by word of mouth, but also under his hand-writing to the said Committees, who were with him at Melton Mowbery, and intreated Colonell Gell that hee would send some fforces to Lancashire and Cheshire, and soe to make a randezvouz, whither hee would come with all speed. Upon this, Colonell Gell sent Major Mollanus, with his horse and dragoones, which were about three hundred and fifty, towards Leeke; as they were marching towards Staffordshire, they had intelligence that the Earl of Newcastle's fforces were falne uppon the Morelanders in Hartington; then they hastened towards them as fast as they could; but before they could attagne thither, they had taken all the ffoott, being about two hundred and forty; and the horse rann all away; which prisoners Colonell Gell afterwards released. And Newcastle's horse marching towards Leek, Mollanus fell uppon them, routed them, and tooke about thirty-five, and slew some five officers, and soe went on to Leek: where the inhabitants, before their coming, were ready to leave their houses and outrunn the towne; and there they were drawing altogether; and Major Mollanus continued their with his fforces fourteen days, all that while noe ayde came to him till the enemy pillaged to the very gates of Derby; and hearing that Sir Thomas Ffairefax was cleane retreated towards Peeterborrough, and noe hopes of his coming to them, Major Mollanus was forced to retreate to Derby with his fforces, without expectation of any ayde at all. And in his retreate, hee tooke att Ashborne twenty-six prisoners, of the Earle of Newcastle's fforces.

In the interim the Earle of Newcastle's fforces sett uppon Wingfield Mannor, in Dec. 7, 1643, and tooke it within some four dayes, because they could have no assistance of any; but yet Colonell Gell's horses and dragoones hardly rested; and in one day they tooke two troopes of horse, with their collours, in Wingfield towne, two captaynes and forty prisoners, within ten dayes after, they fell uppon the guard of Newcastle, at Kilborne, and tooke one Major Wheeler, with ninety prisoners, all horsed, and their collours; a man paynted, and standing with a goold-axe under a greene tree, with this motto: rout and branch; which collours were afterwards sent to his excelencie, with many other collours of horse and ffoott, and soe by him presented to the parliament. As soone as the body of Newcastle's fforces were gone, Colonell Milward, with his regiment, saddled themselves on this side Bakewell; Colonell Eyre att Chatesworth, and att his owne house in the Peake; Colonell Fitzherbert at South Wingfield and Tissington; Colonell Ffretyvisle, at his owne house and Scarsdale: Colonell Harpur, of Little Over, fortefied Burton bridge, whither Colonell Gell sent his Major Mollanus, the 6th of January, 1643, with some of his fforces, and tooke the towne and bridge, with all his whole regiment, horse and ffoott, except Colonell and Leiftennant Colonell, who rann away in the night; hee tooke withall, the major, six captaynes, and eight other officers, with five hundred common souldyers, without any loss of our side but five of the enemy slayne at the entrance of the bridge.

And this day being the 5th of February, 1644, Colonell Gell and his fforces are before King's Mills, which Hastings fortefied, while the Earle of Newcastle's fforces were in the countrey; which King's Mills Colonell Gell tooke by storme, with about two hundred prisoners and soe many armes. Within six or seven dayes after, Colonell Gell having intelligence how the enemy at Bakewell and Tissington hall met every day at Ashborne, hindred the passage, and kept off the countrey people from the markett, sent Major Sanders with five hundred horse and dragoones thither, to cleare the passage; the enemy understanding that our men quartered at Ashborne, drew all the fforces they could together, thinking to surprise them: but our men having intelligence that the enemy was approaching, drew all our dragoones into the lanes and hedges, and charged them: and our horse falling on the reare of them, routed them all and pursued them to the towne of Tissington, and tooke one hundred and seventy prisoners, and many of them slayne. After this defeate they left Tissington and Bakewell, and went some to Ffetchvile and some to Chatesworth house, and some to Bolsover and Wingfeild Mannor.

On the 24th February, 1644, by an especiall command from the Parliament, Colonell Gell sent all his horse and dragoones towards Newarke, under the command of Sir John Meldrum, where they continued about a month, that Prince Rupert raysed the seidge, and in that conflict Colonell Gell lost about two hundred horse and dragoones, with their arms, and the men all stript to their very skin, contrary to all articles of agreement.

After Prince Ruperts returne from Newarke to Ashby-de-la-Zouch, Colonell Gell had intelligence that some of his horse were come over the river Dove, and were plundering some townes about Egginton; he presently sent all his horse out towards Egginton heath, Captayne Rhoades being chief commander thereof. As soone as they came to the heath, the enemy appeared above six hundred strong, and ours but about three hundred and fifty; whereuppon, Colonell Gell having intelligence of the enemyes strength, sent presently Major Mollanus out with four hundred ffoott, towards Egginton heath, to lye in the lanes wayting, least his horse should bee forced to retreate, that they might be ready to fall uppon the enemy if they should pursue them; but before the ffoott came neare them, our horse most valiently had routed them, and driven them into Trent river, where many were drowned and slayne, and two hundred taken prisoners. In the beginning of April, 1644, Colonell Gell having order from the Parliament that forty peeces of ordinance were coming from London to Peeterborrough for him, and that hee should bee carefull to fetch them, with a good convoy; because the enemy being then very strong at Newarke and Ashby-de-la-Zouch, and had open passage to Grantham and Stamford, sent Major Mollanus with five hundred horse and dragoones towards Leicester, with a letter to my Lord Grey, that if their were any danger hee would assist them; presently after they came to my Lord Grey, hee drew them to a randezvouz within three miles of Leicester, with all his horse and dragoones in a body, having intelligence how the enemy were drawing towards Leicestershire from Banbury, Bridgenorth, Dudley and Litchfield, to meet them of Ashby-de-la-Zouch; my Lord commanded them to draw six miles westward towards Tamworth, to the enemyes randezvouz, where they tarried some four dayes; and soe the enemy, hearing of their beinge their, their designe was frustrated. Then my Lord Grey commanded Major Mollanus to march with his horse and dragoones towards Peeterborrough, their to receive his charge; promising that hee would sent his scoutts towards Newarke, and if any of them would stirr, hee would presently bee in the reare of them; and soe Major Mollanus marched safely to Peeterborrough and brought the ordinance to Derby; presently after, there were letters sent from Sir William Brereton to Colonell Gell, how that Prince Rupert was past into the north to assist the Earle of Newcastle against my Lord of Manchester, my Lord Ffairefax and the Scotts, and that hee had order from the Parliament to pursue them, to assist our side with all the fforces hee could procure; soe that Colonell Gell sent him presently three hundred horse and dragoones, and Captayne Rhoades commander in cheife over them.

Within a moneth after, my Lord Grey and Colonell Gell appointed their randezvouz neare Wildon fferry, which lyeth in Leicestershire, where the enemy had made a strong ffort, and had above three hundred men in it for hindering the passage over Trent; and soe immediately environed the ffortt and planted there ordinance and the next day made ready to storme it; but the enemy seeing their resolution, cried out presently, quarter for their lives, and soe they all yielded themselves prisoners; the ffortt demolished, my Lord Grey marched towards Leicester, and Colonell Gell to Derby. Soe hee sent his horse and dragoones to quarter close by Ashby-de-la-Zouch, and by that meanes tooke many prisoners, and they durst noe more sturr to rob carriers.

Within tenn dayes after, Colonell Gell sent to Nottingham to Governor Hutchinson and Colonell Thornough, for their assistance to beleaguer Wingfield Manor, because it was as great an annoyance to Nottinghamshire as to Derbyshire; Colonell Thornough presently sent his Major with troopes of horse and met Colonell Gell, who brought all his ffoott and horse with him (except two companyes of ffoott which hee left in Derby) within a mile of Wingfield, and presently invironed the Mannor house; and about ten days after, Colonell Hutchinson sent two hundred ffoott. After they had layne fifteen dayes there, Colonell Gell had intelligence how the enemy at Litchfield, Tutbury, Ashby-de-la-Zouch, and other garrisons, were gathering their fforces together about Burton, for to relieve the Mannor; he presently sent Sanders, Major of his horse, with all the horse and dragoones towards them, and to have an eye to Derby; our horse coming neare the enemy, and hearing that Colonell Eyre, his regiment, lay in Boylston church, our dragoones dismounted, and surprised the whole regiment in the church: and soe tooke men, arms, collours, and all without loss of one man on either side. And hearing that Colonell Bagort, governor of Litchfield, was with all his horse and ffoott at Burton, marching towards the randezvouz, our men presently left a guard of dragoones on the prisoners in the church, and marched with their horse towards Burton, and assaulted the enemy; and after two or three hott encounters, beate them cleare out of the towne, where there were five of our side slayne, and seventeen of the enemy, and many of them taken prisoners, and brought backe to Bolyston Church to the other prisoners, which made upp three hundred in all: and soe marched them to Derby, with six ffoott collours and one horse collour, with all their armes; and soe our men and horse returned to the leaguer at Wingfeild Mannor againe; Colonell Gell finding that his ordinance would doe noe good against the Mannor, and understanding that Major Generall Craford had foure great peeces, sent two of his officers unto him, to desire him to send him them for three or four dayes for battering: and in soe doinge hee would doe the countrey good service, because it was a place that could not bee otherwise taken, without they were pined out. Major Generall Craford, desirous to doe the state and countrey good service, came presently with his ordinance and some horse and ffoott thither; and soe wee planted ours and their ordinance together, and after three houres battrey they yielded themselves, being about two hundred and twenty; and soe uppon composision, every one marched to his own home; and soe Major Generall Craford marched towards Lincolne, where the Earle of Manchester quartred, and Colonell Gell to Derby, leaving behind him in the Mannor two ffoott companyes and a troope of horse.

Presently after Colonell Gell had taken Wingfield Mannor, all the enemyes scattered fforces, which were routed in Yorkshire, and belonging to Derbyshire, Leicestershire and Staffordshire, came to Litchfield, Ashby-de-la-Zouch and Tutbury, and began to robb and plunder in Derbyshire and Leicestershire; ffor preventing whereof, Colonell Gell sett upp a garrison at Barton Parke, opposite to Tutbury, in October, 1644, and soe kept Tutbury men in, that they could doe noe hurt to Derbyshire. Leicestersire Committee seeing this, sent to Colonell Gell for his assistance to sett up a garrison at Coleorton, within a mile, and opposite to Ashby-de-la-Zouch. Thereupon hee sent them all the horse and dragoones he could well spare; and soe continued there all the moneth of November, 1644, till it was perfected. The first of December next following, Sir William Brereton sent to Colonell Gell for assistance to beseidge Chester; hee presently sent him six troopes of horse and dragoones, who continued there till the latter end of March.

Within four dayes after, Colonell Rossiter and Governor Hutchinson sent to Colonell Gell for assistance, for an onslought which they had uppon Newarke men; whereupon Sir John sent them all the remaynder of his horse and dragoones, being six troopes; as soone as Nottingham men, Lincolne men, and our men were in the vale of Belvoyer, they presently descryed the enemy, horse and ffoott; charged and routed them, slew many of them, and drove many of them into a brooke, that they were drowned; and Sir Richard Byron, then governor of Newarke, had much a doe to save himself, in running on ffoott to Belvoyer Castle, leaving his perriwicke behind him on the ground, many of them taken prisoners, and our troopes brought with them about thirty good horse to Derby, which made some satesfaction for our losse before Newarke; of this exployt, Colonell Rossiter was Commander in chiefe. About the latter end of December, 1644, the committee of both kingdomes sent an order to Sir John Gell, that hee should send all the horse and dragoones which hee could spare, to the assistance of blocking upp the north side of Newarke, under the command of Colonell Sanders where they tarried till the midst of March. About the beginning of April, 1645, Colonel Gell's horse came backe from Chester: and the very same night, the Governor of Nottingham sent his letter, how Sir Richard Willis, Governor of Newarke, had surprised Nottingham bridge, and that hee entreated all the assistance hee could make, with all speede possabley; the next morning Sir John Gell sent all his horse and dragoones thither; within three and four dayes after, the Governor of Newarke finding that hee could not hould it, came with a good strength, and brought his men off backe to Newarke, soe that their was noe losse in regayning it, because the enemy left it.

In the beginning of May, 1645, the Kinge came to Litchfield and soe to Tudbury, and from thence sett before Leicester, and by storme tooke it. In the meane tyme theire came a letter from the Committee of both

Kingdomes to Colonell Gell, that hee should draw to Nottingham with his horse and dragoones, where they had commanded all the horse and dragoones of Cheshire, Staffordshire, Nottinghamshire, and others to meete at the randezvouz att Nottingham, under the command of Colonell Gell, and hee, with the said fforces to follow the Kinge, what way soever hee marched. As soone as the fforces came together (which was att least fourteen dayes first) Colonell Gell advanced in the meane tyme; the Kinge was routed att Naysby, and his excellence, Sir Thomas Ffairefax, advancing towards Leicester, commanded Sir John Gell to lye with his fforces on the north side of it, and soe the towne of Leicester was surrendered, and afterwards hee dismissed Colonell Gell, and all the fforces that were under his command. Hee was noe sooner come backe to Derby, but their came a letter from the Committee of both Kingdomes that hee should march with his owne horse and dragoones to Coventrey, where they had commanded all the other fforces, which were formerly under his command, to meete him there; and when hee had marched as farr as Synfen Moore, part of his horse began to mutinie for want of money, and turned backe, nevertheless hee marched forwards with two or three troopes, and tarried there tenn dayes, and noebody coming to him hee returned backe again to Derby. Hee was noe sooner come home but Colonell Thornhaugh sent a letter unto him, that Welbecke was surprised by the enemy of Newarke, and that Colonell Ffretchvile was made Governor thereof, and gathered a greate strengeth, and therefore desired him, hee would send him all the assistance hee could for to keepe them in, before they were provided of provision, and that hee would meete them about Wingfeild Mannor. Sir John presently drew all his horse and dragoones together, and marched with them himselfe thither, and delivered them under the command of Colonell Thornhaugh, who tarried their a while and encountred twice or thrice with the enemy, and beate them, and tooke many prisoners. Uppon the Kinge coming to Derbyshire our fforces returned backe to Derby.

In the beginning of September, 1645, there came letters from the Committee of both Kingdomes, that Colonell Gell should keepe five hundred ffoott ready uppon an hower's warning, to marche towards Newarke, under the command of Colonell Generall Poynts, for the blocking upp of Newarke. In the meane tyme Staffordshire men sent unto Colonell Gell, that if hee would assist them with a considerable number of ffoott, they would beseidge Tudbury castle, whereupon hee assured them that hee would assist them with all the fforces hee had, but that as soone as hee received orders from Colonell Generall Poynts, seven hundred of his ffoott must bee ready at his command at an hower's warning, because he had received such orders from the Parliament, for the blocking upp of Newarke. Notwithstanding hee sent his Leiftennant Colonell with four hundred ffoott to the rendezvouz, within a mile of Tudbury, where Staffordshire officers and ours mett together, and held a councell of warr, and found that it would bee at least a moneth's work, and therefore neither they nor wee could tarry so long about it, because of our former command, and for storming it, it was impossible, and soe returned to our severall garrisons.

Within two dayes after oure returne, the Kinge came with three thousand horse to Tudbury, and from thence to Ashborne, where our horse fell in the reare of them, and tooke a Major, much esteemed by the Kinge, and twenty-five prisoners, which Major was afterwards exchanged for one Major Gibb, who was Major over the horse in the associated countyes, by the Earle of Manchester's letter, and soe the Kinge marched through the High Peake to Doncaster.

The latter end of September, 1645, the Governor of Welbecke having gotten good strength by the Kinge coming that way, came to Derbyshire with three hundred horse and dragoones to set upp a garrison in Chatsworth, and one Colonell Shallcross for Governor there, Colonell Gell having intelligence thereof sent presently Major Mollanus, with four hundred ffoott to repossess the house; and having layne their fourteen dayes, and hearing of the demolishing of Welbecke, Bolsover and Tickhill castles, was commanded by Colonell Gell to return to Derby.

About the same tyme Sir William Brereton sent to Colonell Gell for his assistance to beseidge Chester, hee presently sent him six troopes of horse and dragoones, where they continued till it was taken, and returned to Derby in February next after.

And within tenn dayes after Sir William sent for them againe to the beseidging of Litchfield, whither they went, and tarried their till the surrender thereof.

The 28th of October, 1645, Colonell Generall Poynts sent to Sir John Gell, according to the Parliament's order, that hee should send him his fforces to the randezvouz at Belvoyer in the vale, hee presently sent Major Mollanus with five hundred and twenty ffoot thither, who remayned under his command with one Captayne Leiftennant Drinkwater alone, till Newarke was surrendered, being the 8th of May, 1646, and then the said Major received order, from the Grand Committee before Newarke, to returne backe to Derby with his fforces and artillery.

In this service that wee were under Colonell Generall Poynts first storming of Belvoyer outworkes about the castle, of Colonell Gell's men eleven were slayne, and twenty-seven wounded; and for their service and valor in storming the said workes, the Parliament bestowed £40, amongst Derby souldyers to drinke.

And at Stoake, the 1st of January, 1645, four slayne and thirty wounded, whereof the Major's own Leiftennant was one, and three sergeants, and twenty-seven taken prisoners. Which skirmish continued from three of the clocke in the morning till six, that the enemy were beaten backe, having seventy-two of their men wounded and slayne, whereof was one Captayne

Fforster; the enemy were one thousand ffoott and four hundred horse strong, and wee, from Derby and Nottingham could not at that instant make five hundred ffoott betwixt us, and most of our horse ran away, but Captayne Pendocke who was sore wounded and taken prisoner.

In this skirmish Derbyshire ffoott stood most valiantly and courageously too it, soe that as soone as it was day, Colonell General Poynts gave them many thanks in the open feild, where they stood in battalio, for their courage and valor. And before Newarke wee left seven men and one wounded.

For all the aforesaid severall good services, done by Colonell Gell, his officers and souldyers, the horsemen were disbanded with £4.6s. apeece, and the ffoott with £1.6s. apeece, and the officers never a penny to this day, being most of them two years' pay in arreare, and therefore lett the world judge whether wee are well rewarded or noe; but the reason is, as I suppose, because the greater part of our Committee were of the Kinge's side till after the battell at Yorke, and especially our Sub-committee of array.

Gresley's Account

A true account of the raysing and imployeing of one foote regiment under Sir John Gell from the beginning of October, 1642.

When the setters up, as wel as the lookers on, were wearye of the standard's longer stay at Nottingham, the king's first march was to Derby, the trayned bands of the country being commanded to attend him, which they did, and were disarmed for reward. This new army left such a force behynd them, that a couple of base strangers, one Dennis, and Ballard, papists in religion, and beggars by fortune, for their bouldness to settle themselves at Wyrksworth about the myddle of the county, upon pretence to raise souldyers for the king, began to robb and plunder without controule, though at that tyme we had four earles, one baron, and dyvers knights, and gentlemen, al liveing amongst us; with these two strangers dyvers of our owne county soone joyned, some popeishe in theyre religion, others of lewd lyfe and lyttle fortune, wherefore to prevent the miserable condition that our country was like to fall into, and the better to enable Sir John Gell to raise a regiment of foote, according to his excellency the Earle of Essex' commission, to him for a Colonell, Sir John, with his brother, Mr. Thomas Gell, his Leifetennant-Colonell, went about the end of September unto Hull to Sir John Hotham, by whose letter to his sonne, at Cawwood castle, were procured one foote company, with which we marched for Derbyshire. And in our way we weare importuned to helpe there at Sheaffeild to suppress a muteny there, which we did, and they lent us ould calivers wyth rotten stocks and rusty barrells, useless to them and of little service to us; for which they seised and took afterwards sixty good muskets of ours, as they came from Hull.

During our absence Sir Francis Wortley, with a company of fellowes fyt for such a leader, with horses and arms, stoln from honest men, came and joyned with them at Wyrksworth; by which union of theirs they conceived themselves masters of the county, and, in confidence thereof, disposed of other men's houses and estates, for their wynter quarter; when, unexpected of them, Sir John Gell appears at Chesterfield, as much to the content of the wel affected as to the amasement of these robbers; within fewe dayes after Colonell Gell's first appearing at that towne, the Earls of Devonshire and Chesterfield together with the then Hygh Sheriffe, Sir John Harpur of Cawke, Sir John Harpur of Swarkston, Sir John Fitzherbert of Norbury, Sir Edward Vernon, Sir Simon Every, and divers other gentlemen of our county, mett at Tutbury and sent a threatening letter to Colonell Gell for his comeing with forces into that countie, to which he returned an answer by their messenger, that it seemed strange they should growe so quickly jealous of hym, theyre owne countrieman, wel known to them, and that had no other end, then the cleareing of his county from theeves and robbers, to mayntaine the lawes of the land and liberties of the subject, according to the ordynance of Parliament, and yet for a long tyme they could suffer Sir Francis Wortley and others to robb and spoyle without interruption; after this answer wee presently marched to Wyrkesworth, drove Wortley and that crew out of the county, and then went straight to Derby; where our sudden appearing prevented the designs of our malignant countriemen, for whilst they were consulting how to raise forces to oppose us, and shareinge every man's proportion, how many to mayntaine, our being at Derby in the mydst of them crossed all; what could not be done by force, they then endeavoured to effect by treatie, desireinge the Colonell to give them meeting, but to leave his strengthe behyned, a request too symple for us to yeild unto. Sir George Gresley was now joyned with us, the onely gentleman of qualety in this county that cordyally appeared to be on our side; Wortley returned into the Peake againe, whom wee suddenly sent away, with such a fear that he troubled us no more.

Afterwards our countrie gentlemen desired another meeting at Etwall; wyther Sir George Gresley, Leiftennant-Colonell Gell, Major Saunders, and Mr. Hallowes went; who quickly perceived that nothing would suite with the designes of the malignant, but the dissolving of our forces, wee resolved to keepe together.

From that meeting Sir John Harpur, of Swarkeston, went to Rixham, and procured the assistance of Generall Hastings with some troopes of horse, but before their comeinge the Earle of Chesterfield had sent for his sonne Ferdynando from Oxford, who brought with him a troupe of horse, his father mett hym at Burton, and theyre publiqueley in the towne swoare that within a few dayes he would have Derby, but this was nether the first, nor last tyme the Earle's oath hath benn broaken. But the better to serve ourselves wee presently marched to the Earle's house, Bretby, then furnished with about one hundred and twenty souldiers, horse and foote, well provided of all necessaries; the house was too strong for our small ordynance, but our foote came desperately up to the walls, which the Earle perceiving presently fled with his sonne and al his horse; we tooke the house and should have donne no more hurt, but only taken the armes and ammunition, if the Countess would have given the common souldiers £20 to drink, which she refusing, part of the house was plundered, to which act the souldiers were more inclined, when they understoode that some of their fellowes taken prisoner at the first onsett had received hard usage, some of them having had the honour to be beaten by the Earle himself, whom his servants had first disarmed, and then held fast from styrring; but night comeing on, the wayes foule, and we haveing no nearer quarter then

Burton, were forced to make hast away.

Our neighbours at Nottingham were now desirous to raise some forces, which good work we were willing to advance, gave Captaine Whyte leave to goe with his dragooners to them, who at first came to us with about one hundred well armed. By this tyme Generall Hastings was seated at Ashby, which place he fortifyed, and much annoyed both the counties of Leicester and Derby, whereupon the Lord Grey sent to us to joyne with him against Ashby, at the same tyme Sir William Bruerton came from London with some few horse, and we altogether went against Ashby. Our regiment was appoynted to fall upon the towne, we beate the enemy out of the workes, tooke the towne and forced them to retyre into the mannor house and church; but presently after the Lord Grey, our commander in cheife, had false intelligence of the comeing of Prince Rupert, which he too easily believed, and called us off, and so saved Hastings and the house, which otherwise had been yielded to us. So apprehensive was his Lordship of Prince Rupert's comeing, that he went straight to Leicester, where Sir William Bruerton and he stayed upon theyre owne occasions until they lost us and the towne £500 which was but a small loss in respect of what damage Hastings hath since done us; who hath ever been a thorn in our sydes. Upon Christmas Day, presently after, we sent more of our forces to Nottingham for a designe against Newarke; but false intelligence defeated that design also; for those that should have joyned with us, beleived the enemies forces to be farre greater then in trueth they were; and so held back theyre assistance; yet our men continued at Nottingham, sett out theyre workes, and stayed there untyll those works were advanced. Whylst part of our forces weare thus imployed att Nottingham, Hastings with Sir John Harpur came to Swarkeston, Sir John's horse and I beganne to fortifie there; but we easily perceived how dangerous it was to suffer such neighbours so neare us; we went presently against them, they quitt the house at our fyrst comeing, but kept the bridge for a tyme; which in regard of the river of Trent which runnes under it, and that we could approache it but one way, where they had made a strange bulwarke, the attempt was difficult, yet the valour of our men overcame it, and drove both the commanders and souldiers out of our countrey; and from thence Captain Munday with his company went into Yorkshire, at the intreaty of Sheafeild men, where he stayed untill he had effected what they desired.

The Morelanders in Staffordshire next desired our ayde against Stafford, and they promised more forces to joyne with us, then was in theire power to performe. We sent our ordynance and men to Uttoxeter, but finding our forces less than wee expected and the garryson in Stafford greater then was at fyrst reported, for theyre were new supplies come thyther from Shrewsbury, we retourned to Derby, but sent some forces to Leeke to trayne and exercise theyre men, of which at that tyme they stoode in great neede. Not long after we placed a garryson in Burton-upon-Trent, the better to secure that towne, and a greate part of our country. We were agane commanded to joyne with others against Newarke, under the commande of Major Ballard, wyther we sent our forces under the command of Major Mollanus; which did theyre parts, for we beate the enemie out of theyre workes, and placed our coulors upon them; and when there was no other expectation but of rakeing the towne, instead of being seconded we were called off, for some secret reason, which our commanders could never yet truely understand. Whylest part of our forces were thus engaged at Newarke, Captain Fox came post from Lichefeild, and brought the sadd news of the noble Lord Brooke's death, whereupon our Colonell went immediatelie with the Captaine to Lichefeild, and kept together those forces ready to disband; he continued the seige, tooke the close, with the Earl of Chesterfeild and dyverse other prysoners. They after joyned with Sir William Bruerton who brought some horse and went against Stafford, but the enemie being farre stronger then was expected, the Earle of Northampton with above one thousand horse came out of Stafford, and fell upon our men on a heath within two myles of Stafford; at the very first encounter all our horse fled, except about two hundred and forty of the Lord Brooke's reformader troupe, who behaved themselves all very gallantly. Our Collonell quitt his horse, and went to the foote, being then in great feare and disorder, many of them readie to rune, and standing with theyre pykes advanced; the Colonell, with his owne hands, put downe theyre pykes, encouraged both them and the musquetyers, who were all disorderly, crowded together; he speedely gott them into order and gave the enemie such a vollie of shott upon theyre chardge, that they first wheeled, and much discouraged by the death of the Earle of Northampton and Captaine Middleton, with dyvers others, gentlemen and officers, they all presently fledd; at the same instant Captain Bowyer with one foote company, came very valiantly and joyned with our force; the same horse that fledd, used meanes to discourage hym in this fyght; the horse, al but the reformader troupe, and all the Captains of foote, except Captain Thomas Willoughby, left the feyld; yet we gott the victorie, brought away the dead body of the Earle of Northampton, theyre generall, and had the pylladge of the feild. When that was donne, and noe enemie apeared of five houers after, wee went with our weary men to Chartley, where those that left us in the fyght returned to us againe.

By our garison and friends about Chesterfield, we were often pressed to come against the Lord Deincourt, to satisfie theyre reasonable request, the Leieutennant-Colonell, Major Mollanus and Captain Saunders, were sent thyther with two peeces of ordynance; that Lord was summoned, refused to yeild, and obstinately held out for a long tyme, yet at last he came forth and pawned both his fayth and honour to performe certaine easie conditions, in confidence whereof, we returned to Chesterfield, but that Lord, contrary to the articles, went early the next morning to Newarke, which perfidious dealing of his, our very adversaries have since, in some measure, revenged, for the garrison at Balsover pillaged the house, and those of Newarke caused hym to unburye his money, and to bestow it in the maintenance against God and the kingdome; his lands, the cavaliers have leased, because they know not how to take it, which cannot be better bestowed then towards the dischardge of publique engagements; and so then that lumpe of fleshe will bee nether for service of Kinge nor Parliament.

Not long after the plundering, Prynce Rupert came to Lichefeild, and like a conqueror thought to take that in his way, his principal designe being for Derbie, and the suppressing of our forces, to which, besides other motives, he was ernestly importuned by many of our cheife countrymen. Whilst this Prince lay at the seige of Lychfeild we mended our workes, and called in other garrisons expectinge our own turne next; when al our owne forces were together, though we weare unable to releive, yet wee pytied the condition of these brave men beseiged at Lichfeild, we often importuned the Lord Grey to joyne with us for theyre releife, which if his Lordship had donne we had eyther releived the place or dyed in the attempt. This Prince after a long seige, and with loss of many men, tooke the close at Lichfeild, but instead of comeing on to Derbie, he returned back to Oxford; but left a garison at Burton, which the Lord Grey and wee tooke presently after, and there wee placed Captaine Sanders with his company.

Whilst these things were in actinge, the Earle of Newcastle grewe powerfull in the North. He came with a strong armie and besieged Rotheram, the Leifetennant was then at Chesterfield, onely with two foote companies, and two small peeces of ordynance; and being ernestly importuned by Sheaffeild men, and others, to joyne with them and some promised forces from the Lord Fayrfax, he went with a purpose to have joyned with them, and endeavour the raiseing of that seige; but, as he was upon his marche, a couple of our owne souldyers, that had been in Rotheram, dureing the seidge, and found meanes to escape, by takeing up armes for the enemie, came and told him the towne was taken, Sheaffeild castle quitt, most of the honest men fledd, and not any hope of help from the Lord Fayrefax. The Leifetennant-Collonell, with those two companies and ordynance, returned to Derbie, which the enymie might easily have cut off, if he had knowne in what condition we were. Newcastle's army was now victorious, he came on into our country, miserably plunders, and takes all before hym, leavies greate summies of money, and raiseth more men by the commission of aray; we were again threatened, and expected daylie to be besieged, and, to speak ingenuously, we never were in more danger than at that instant, therefore we called in our garison to assist us; but Captaine Saunders, who had one hundred and eighty of our foote, well armed, and some horse, raised in our county, and intended principally for this countries service, under our regiment, he refused in this our extremity to come unto us, yet he sent us his coulours and commission, but kept our men, armes, and horses; all which he turned over to Colonell Houghton; and was for that good service made his liefetennant-colonell. It pleased God to preserve us, and the Northern Popish army, in the height of theire pryde, were suddenly called back by the Lord Fayrefax, his judicious and valiant takeing of Wakefeild. The generall randevouse, now at Nottingham, now . . . . whyther we were commanded, and stayed there with our forces seven weekes, dureing which tyme Warton house was beseiged, and our men put upon the service well beate the enemie out of theyre workes, and were likely to take the house in a short tyme, when, upon a rumor of the Queene's forces comeing towards Newarke, we were suddenly commanded of. Once, afterwards, the Queene's army faced Nottingham, and had the other commanders beene as forward to fight as ours, wee had then put it to the fortune of a battell; but it was otherwise resolved, and our horse went presently after to Leicester, with the Lord Grey and Colonell Cromwell, upon pretence to fetch Colonell Pargrave's regyment of foote; but neyther those foote, nor our horse, came any more to Nottingham. The Leifetenant-Collonell, Captaine Swetnam, and Captaine Mellaar, with those forces left at Derbie, beseiged and took Sir Richard Fleetwood and his house in Staffordshire, being one of the strongest places in that county, exceeding well provided of all necessaries, and manned with such a company of obstinate papists, and resolute theeves, as the like were hardly to be found in the whole kingdome. In the absence of our horse from Nottingham, the Queene passeth by to Ashby, her army assaults, takes, and plunders Burton, carries away the commanders and souldyers prisoners, yet since we redeemed Leifetennant-Colonell Saunders, being confident of his promise to serve faithfully hereafter in this countrie, wee consented that he should bee major of that regiment of horse, for raising whereof his exellency hath lately granted a commision to Sir John Gell, as collonell.

During the Queene's stay at Ashby, Hastings laboured exceedingly to have theyre forces come against Derby, but all in vaine, for our regiment was now returned from Nottingham; and wee were but weake before, fortunately supplied with twenty barrells of pouder, three hundred muskets, sixty carbines, and sixty cases of pystolls, being the free gyft of the honourable House of Commons, and which wee shall ever gratefully acknowledge, and without which we had been in more danger; for though we writt to Nottingham for some foote, they haveing then about two thousand theire, and theyre danger past with the Queene, yet would they not afford us any, which was the principall cause of the loss of Burton. For, had wee been able, as wee desired to have sent some foote thyther, that towne had been saved. Presently after the Queene left Ashby, wee beseiged Tutbury castle, and in it Hastings, with many of his best commanders; and when they were brought to great extremety, not able to hold out much longer, Major Freton would needes be gone with Nottingham horse, and so caused us to raise our seige when that castle could not have held out two daies longer. Presently after Sir John Meldrum sent to us to joyne with the Lord Willoughby and hym against Newarke; our forces went and were neare the towne. But upon intelligence of greate supplies come thither from Gainsborough, that enterprise was defeated. The garison at Nottingham presently after was removed thence, and we were againe sent for, and went to Leeke, whilst they victuled the castle, and removed such goods thyther as was thought convenient; not longe after our cominge home the enemie took Nottingham towne, and possessed themselves of it, the castle being in a manner beseiged, they sent to us for releife, many of theyre souldyers being hydd in the towne and in danger to be left, unless we presently releived them. We sent Major Mollanus instantly, and he joyned with three troopes of horse from Leicester; with these he entered the towne, beate the enemie thence, though they were more in number then our men, killed many of the enimie, took one hundred and sixty prisoners, redeemed of souldiers, and divers other honest, one thousand four hundred. About ten daies after the committee of Nottingham sent to us againe for helpe, in regard the enimy had fortifyed at the bridge, and cut off all passage to the towne on that syde, our souldiers went againe, and after some tyme we beate the enemie from the bridge, which was of such importance that the governour of the castle professed to Major Mollanus, that unless our souldyers would stay and take the bridge we would quitt the castle, lett the Parliament doe with him what they would. When they had donne this, we went about gatherying some money from our souldiers, and being upon the borders of Yorkshire, we had intelligence of the Marquiss of Newcastle's army, by reason of the seige of Hull and the great discouradgment of many of his party, after the victory at Hornecastle, and the takeing of Lincolne, some principall men retireing to their houses, purposely to make their peace, of which we gave notice to others, but nothing was donne saveing the loss of a fyne opportunitie to have constrained the Marquiss of Newcastle's sick army, within the wasted parts of Yorkshyre, which army was quietly permitted to retreat fyrst in Nottinghshyre, and after to wast and destroy a greate parte of Derbyshire, to the utter doeing of many honest men, and the inricheing of many popish theeves; but before Newcastle's army came into Derbyshire, Sir Thonmas Fayrfax was at Nottingham with his horse, our colonell went to hym, to bring hym to Derby, whyther Sir Thomas came, but first he had a meeting, unknown both to the colonell and committies, with some of our countrymen, at Wingfeild mannor; when Sir Thomas was comen to us, we desired hym to quarter nere Tutbury with his horse, and to beseige it with our foote; but his answer was he could not stay, and within few dayes he went into the Peake, and there had conference with other of our countrymen, and writt to Derby that two of the committes might meet hym at Chesterfeild on Saturday following, whyther the Leifetannant-Colonell and Mr. Hallowes went, and one hundred and thirty of our musquetiers mett them that night, and more were apoynted to come thyther on Monday followeing; but in the meane tyme, on Sonday in the afternoone, some of the Marquiss of Newcastle's horse appeared within two myles of the towne, and gave an alarum. Sir Thomas Fayrfax adviseth with his owne men, and resolves to be gone; the Leifetenant-Colonell and Mr. Hallowes were forced to goe of a sudden, and ride that night to quitt our garison at Wingerworth, and another att Chattsworth; shortly after we sent to Sir Thomas at Nottingham, to informe hym of the enemies strength, which was not greate, and to advise with hym what course to be taken; he promised help if we stood in neede, but in the meane tyme removed further from us, to Melton, we sent two of the committee to hym, namely, Mr. Hallowes and Mr. Wygfall; he againe promised us help, but wished us to gett what foote we could from Lancashire, Cheshire and Staffordshyre; to them wee sent and they promised a good body of foote to joyne with us, provided that Sir Thomas would come with his horse, of all which we gave hym notice, and desired his speedy help, in regard the enimie was now farr advanced in our countrye, and miserably oppressed us by plundering, and that illegall commission of array. The better to keepe the foote of our neighbouring counties together, we sent our horse to Leeke, who came thyther fortunately for that county, for, just as the enemie had routed theyre forces, our horse came into them, tooke about twenty of the enimies, caused them to recrute and keepe them afterwards for entring Staffordshyre. Our horse stayed there about a fortnight, in which tyme wee sent severall lettres to Sir Thomas Fayrfax, ernestly desireing his ayd, wee had only promises but no assistance. In the meane tyme the enimy pillaged very neare Derby, and our neighbor countrymen, despayring of any ayd from Sir Thomas Fayrfax, returned home, and so did our horse to us.

After they had quartered about Leeke a fortnight, wee ernestly importuned the Lord Grey for help; he gave us hope by his letters, but left us to ourselves. Wee imployed our horse the best we could, fell upon the enemies quarters, tooke a major, and two troupes, one night; which, with some other dammadg they received from us, made them keepe afterwards a farther distance from Derby. Newcastle's army now beseiged Wyngfeild mannor, the only garison, but this towne, that was left us in the county, which for want of releife, he took by composition. His lordship was often and ernestly importuned to beseige Derby, by our malicious countriemen and Hastings, who proffered all the force that possible he could make; but Newcastle was sufficiently informed of our resolution to defend itt, and could not be drawne to the enterprise by any means they could all make to hym. His business in the Northe now calls hym to Yorke; but he leaves to vex us, his owne garison at Balsover, and six collonells of his owne country, whereof five, namely, Sir John Fytsherbert, Sir John Harpur, Mr. Fretchevile, Mr. Ayre, and Mr. Milward, had such regiments as theire owne interest, backed with the commission of array, and the popeishe party, could raise for them. The sixt colonell, Sir Symon Every, haveing nether men nor armes, and wanting meanes to trouble this county, he went to Oxford to expect the success of the ante-parliament there. Sir John Harpur, with his regiment, beganne to fortifie at Burton, whyther our Major Mollanus with our horse and some dragooners went, fell upon them, tooke theire major, six captaines, many other officers and common souldyers, by which act the whole regiment was spoyled. Within few dayes after Major Sanders went to South Wyngeild with our horse, and theire tooke two captaines and some other officers and souldyers of Sir John Fitsherbert's regiment. In our greatest extremitie Captaine Clarke and Captaine Taylor most unworthely runne away from us, and at the chardge of this county, these commanders went fyrst to Nottingham, where they stayd above one weeke, and were after entertained, when they should have been punished by the Lord Grey, although wee often writ to his Lordship to have sent them to us, but in vaine. Not long before the like slippery part played Captaine Ashenhurst, being captaine of the collonell's own troope, whoe runne away with about forty of our horse, for which worthy service he has since become a major; but whether to the new collonell his brother, or to the wandering Collonell Chadwick, wee certainly knowe not, these two collonells being greate friends, and much together; as in reason they should, for theyre regiment consists of fewe more then that single troope. At the importunitye since of many poore neighbors, that were miserably oppressed by a garison of Hastings his souldyers, at the kings milnes, the collonell went the last weeke and beseiged and tooke it, with the captaine and all the other officers and common souldyers, with some malignant countrymen fledd thyther for safetie. And since then Staffordshire men have beseiged Byddle house, and fearing to have the seige raised by Hastings and our countrymen, desired to lie with our horse in the confines of theyre county, which wee did, and sent our horse and dragooners under Major Saunders to Ashbourne. Our countrymen from Tissington and the Peake drew above three hundred horse and foote together, purposeing to fall upon our men in theire quarters; but ours being readie, mett them at the townsend, killed some, and tooke above one hundred prysoners, with as many horses and armes. Their officers all runne away cowardly, so that the greatest officer wee tooke was but a cornet. Besides the above-mentioned passages, it is impossible to relate our continuall and almost daylie encounters with the Earl of Newcastle's garison at Bolesover and Welbeck, being from time to time supplied from Newark and Yorkshyre, which trouble us on the North syde; and no less Hastings on the South, for he, being generall under the king in six countries, employes of all his witt and power principally against us. Now lett any indifferent and impartial man judge, whether our single regiment of foote have layne idle, and wee had never more, untill of late his excellency granted our collonell another commission to raise a regiment of horse. He that shall consider that Prince Rupert, with his army, came once against us, Newcastle in person twice, and the Queene ernestly pressed, when she lay at Ashbie, the plunder of this towne, offered as a reward to hyr souldiers, and yet we are safe, may easylie conclude, that the hand of God were then our proper strength, and hath protected us; our cheife friends under God were the Parliament, that supplied us in our want, and his excellency the Erle of Essex, who never denied us anything wee writt to hym for, which wee humbly and thankfully acknowledge. For good fortune that wee are not destroyed, wee give God the glory. And others have reason to thank hym too; for let wise men consider if this towne had been lost, and our malignant lords and gentlemen in possession of this place, what had become of our neighbour counties, as also of Lankeshire and Cheshire, when in former extremities, and in greate neede they have found no way to be supplied with ammunition and other necessaries, but what came to them by the way of this towne, and without which they could not possibly subsist.

That the world may know, we nether undertooke the business at first with other men's money, nor have since imployed any man's estate to our own benefit, we profess before God and man, that when we went first to Hull to procure some souldiers to beginne withall, that we had not then any advance money, eyther from the Parliament, our owne country, or any other man or woman whatsoever; but mearly went upon our owne chardges. And that the collonell hath since sould his stock, spent his revenue, and put himselfe into debt, in mayntenance of his cause. And that he never received of any treasurer, towards al his chardges, above £240 and the leifetennant-collonell hath also disbursed and layed out in mayntenance of this cause, a greate part of his estate; and, never yet received one daies pay; so that we are out of purse many hundred pounds, spent mearely in this business. And this we proffess upon the fayth of Christians, and as wee hope for creditt and esteeme among honest men. This our profession we freelie make to take off some base and lying imputations, and not that we are weary of the cause; in mayntenance whereof wee are absolutely resolved to continue and persevere, so long as God shall lende us lives to venter, and estates to spend.

Index